THE
WINDOW
SEAT

Also by Aminatta Forna

Happiness

Ancestor Stones

The Memory of Love

The Hired Man

The Devil That Danced on the Water

AMINATTA FORNA

NOTES FROM A LIFE IN MOTION

THE WINDOW SEAT

Grove Press
New York

Published simultaneously in Canada
Printed in the United States of America

First Grove Atlantic hardcover edition: May 2021

Library of Congress Cataloging-in-Publication data is available for this title.

ISBN 978-0-8021-5858-1
eISBN 978-0-8021-5859-8

Grove Press
an imprint of Grove Atlantic
154 West 14th Street
New York, NY 10011

Distributed by Publishers Group West

groveatlantic.com

21 22 23 24   10 9 8 7 6 5 4 3 2 1

For Maureen Campbell White

Contents

The Window Seat

Here are four words you rarely hear these days: I love to fly. I do. I'm talking about being a passenger on a commercial flight. Whatever emotions attend the journey, whether I am flying for work or pleasure, towards loved ones or away, once in my seat—especially if I am alone and have managed to secure myself a window seat—on seeing the marshaller signalling the plane with orange batons like a tamer before a recalcitrant circus beast, a feeling of ease comes over me. This remains true after the hundreds of flights I have taken. I love the drama of the take off. The improbability of the whole endeavour. A cat jumping is a reversal of gravity—the cat seems to pour itself upwards. An aeroplane is more like a galloping draught horse that, through sheer determination, somehow succeeds in clearing the oncoming fence. Having completed its ponderous journey to the runway, the plane turns its nose to face the long stretch of tarmac. Then comes the bellowing of the engines spooling up. The plane begins to move, slowly at first and then faster, faster. I can judge to the second the moment the nose will lift, the wheels leave the tarmac and we shudder into the air. The plane rises, dips and turns in a new quiet.

In 1967 I took my first flight, of which I remember nothing. I travelled with my mother, sister and brother. We were leaving behind Sierra Leone and my father on our way to my mother's family in Scotland. My father was a political activist, and the mood in the country was taut. He had been arrested, detained and released, but now he was being followed wherever he went. Between them, my parents had decided my mother should leave and take us with her. It would be a year before we saw our father again. Sudden departures and arrivals punctuated my childhood. Looking back, flying and fleeing often amounted to the same thing. Though I was too young in those early days to feel the tension and sadness such departures would one day evince, I imagine I was aware, in some peripheral way, of the drama of our departure, the packing of suitcases, the ferry ride to the airport.

In quieter times we came and went on holiday from school in England, flying without the comfort of either parent. We were unaccompanied minors, which in those days carried a different quality of meaning to that which it does now. I was the owner of a Junior Jet Club member logbook in which I recorded all my flight miles with a fountain pen, which the cabin pressure would cause to leak and so I frequently arrived covered in ink. I'd hand my book to the stewardess (they were all stewardesses in those days), who would carry it forward to be signed by the captain. Sometimes, if we were lucky, the captain would invite us into the cockpit. We would walk the length of the plane in pairs, escorted by a hostess like tiny VIPs.

There in the cockpit, flying felt as effortless as sailing; the plane carried the weightlessness of a boat in water. And whereas the windows in the passenger sections were small and dull, here the sky reached out in all directions, a sensation I have only ever had in the widest of landscapes, in the Australian desert or standing before the view from the Bandiagara Escarpment in Mali. In such places the sky is godlike. To fly is to be enfolded into that power. You can do nothing but fall silent. Swimming is as close as humans get to the sensation of flying as birds do. Once, scuba diving, I swam over the edge of an underwater cliff, and below me the seabed fell away some thousand or more feet. Although I was no deeper and in no danger, I felt suddenly afraid and swam back to where I could see the ocean floor.

A few months ago, I was in Heathrow's Terminal Three, and I passed a place so familiar it put a sudden squeeze on my heart. A staircase, an empty space, the marbled floor of the terminal building, that was all there was to it. It took me a moment to realise what was missing: a cordon, maybe six or eight chairs in rows facing another chair upon which an air hostess sat. This was the place where we, the unaccompanied minors, waited to be escorted to our gates. Now the cordon and chairs are gone, the carriers who operated the international flights out of Britain, BOAC (British Overseas Airways Corporation) and British Caledonian (which flew out of Gatwick), ceased operations decades before, and their successor, British Airways, announced in 2016 that they would no longer accept unaccompanied minors.

To fly alone as a child was my first taste of what it might feel like to be on my own in the world. The orphaned or lost child is a trope of children's literature: Cinderella, Anne of Green Gables, Tom Sawyer, Oliver Twist, Mowgli, Mary in *The Secret Garden*, Peter Pan, Harry Potter, Nemo. The young heroes and heroines are unleashed into the enormity of the world, and must prove their courage and resilience as they find home or simply a way to survive.

The unaccompanied minor was a legacy of Empire: the children of colonial officers sent from Kenya, Tanganyika, Ceylon, Hong Kong and India to be educated at boarding school in Britain. In the early days of Empire, the children would have travelled by ship and they probably would have visited their parents only once a year, if at all. Air travel changed that, allowing more frequent visits. BOAC became Britain's national carrier and was created out of the merger of Imperial Airways and another national airline, the first British Airways. During the Second World War, BOAC was tasked with keeping Britain connected to her colonies and the airline continued to maintain those routes after independence.

I was a legacy of Empire as well. But for the Berlin Conference of 1885, which marked the end of the Scramble for Africa and at which the imperial ambitions of the European nations were formalised, my parents would never have met. Africa was stripped of her autonomy and decades of colonial rule followed. After the Second World War, Britain, penniless and under pressure from the United States, handed her colonies their independence with growing haste. Anthems were composed, flags designed, various royals dispatched to oversee the ceremonies at which the Union Jack was lowered. That was the easy part. One among many problems was that there was nobody to run these new states, all of which required lawyers, accountants, engineers, doctors. So, in the years preceding independence, young men and women from the colonised countries were granted scholarships to study in Britain. They were the Renaissance Generation, so named by the writer Wole

Soyinka, a generation who came of age at the same time as their countries. One of them was my father. At a reception hosted by the British Council in Aberdeen he met a local girl who would become his wife and my mother. Through my parents, and later my mother's remarriage to a UN diplomat, I had an unusual exposure to large parts of the world. In my family are represented the histories and nations of Britain, Sierra Leone, Jamaica, Iran, Denmark, China, New Zealand and Canada.

Universal Aunts was founded in 1921 with the primary purpose of escorting unaccompanied minors to and from airports and train stations on their way back to boarding school. I had various guardians in my time, but I certainly stayed with a Universal Aunt more than once. The company was founded by Gertrude Maclean, Aunt Gertie to the seven nephews and nieces she had living in different parts of the Empire and whom she would meet from the plane and drop at school. At first, she ran Universal Aunts out of a room next to a bootmaker in Chelsea. Restrictions on the lease meant that they could not work in the afternoons, so Gertrude and her business partner used to meet their gentlewomen clients in the powder room of the Ladies' in a nearby department store. They still exist, Universal Aunts; their website tells the story of Gertrude Maclean. And they still care for children.

The end of Empire didn't mean the end of children travelling alone to and from the British Isles, because the practise of sending their children home to boarding school was already well established among British expatriates. And it was a practise that rubbed off onto some of the colonised people. My father disliked everything about British colonial rule, but a British education he judged to be excellent and he was, for as long as I can remember, obsessed by the idea that all his children should have one. He had been the only child in his family to receive a Western education, in a deal allegedly struck between the paramount chief and the headmaster of the new mission school which had been built in his district and to whose strangeness people were reluctant to commit their children. The chief and the headmaster agreed that each family was to send one child to school. My father, whose mother had died when he was a child, was elected to be sent by my grandfather's other wives. From there he won a scholarship to Bo School, the so-called Eton of the Protectorate (of Sierra Leone), and thence to Britain. He wanted the same for us. I wept and begged, but he was inflexible, and he put every cent he earned into providing it, though it meant we never owned our own home. I suppose, too, that we were safer at boarding school in England than we might have otherwise been amid the political unrest that affected so much of life in Sierra Leone, though that thought did not occur to me until my adult years.

There were consolations. To fly as an unaccompanied minor was to enter a topsy-turvy world where children were, for once, the most important people. *We* boarded first and had our own reserved rows, always aft, close to the galleys and the staff. *We* were served our meals ahead of all the other passengers, and *we* were given tuck boxes of games, colouring books, comics, pencils and, inevitably, a die-cast model Boeing 747 or a DC-10. The flight crew became our surrogate parents. The stewardesses were our mothers, only more patient and more elegant than our real mothers. These Stepford mothers possessed bright smiles, soothing voices and a limitless supply of snacks. They never ignored us, rather came whenever we called. The uniformed captain already looked like a hero, he commanded three hundred tons of aircraft and two hundred passengers. He did not bother much with us until after take-off, when his smooth voice sounded over the tannoy: 'This is your captain speaking.' And we raised our heads to listen. For six hours we lived inside the perfect patriarchy.

Once, our plane was delayed and we nearly missed our connecting flight. Where were we? Somewhere in Europe; for some reason I think it might have been Munich. We went through a phase of flying Lufthansa, which must at that time have started flying the Freetown route. They gave good gifts but forced us to wear our travel documents in a plastic pouch around our necks. A stewardess rushed us from the plane through a back door, down passages closed to the public. At one point we descended stairs, passed through a door that led onto the tarmac and under the noses of three parked planes. A locked door meant we had to turn back. The stewardess left us while she went, I think, to get a key or someone to unlock the door. Then we were in the stewardesses' changing room, filled with smoke and perfume, where the women went to unpin their chignons, or pin them up, to make up their faces and mend their stockings. It was like the dressing room at the Follies. A hostess came in and slipped off her shoes and jacket and then removed her blouse. As she passed the three of us, she asked another of the women what we were doing there. She had Anne Bancroft's mouth and eyes. She stroked us on the cheek one by one, looking at us as with amused curiosity as though we were gifts left by an admirer.

Another time we became stranded in Charles de Gaulle Airport. I must have been ten or eleven. The usual systems failed, which sometimes happened when one airline was meant to hand us over to another, and we ended up waiting twenty-three hours for our flight, with no money and only the vouchers we had been given to exchange for food. We met a brother and a sister, then a girl on her own, then other unaccompanied minors, until we were a group of some eight or ten children. We raced through the airport, dodging the other travellers; in a cafe we pooled our vouchers to see what food we could buy and, at one point, we tried to persuade a man at a nearby table to give us money in exchange for some of them so we could buy toys and chocolate. When we arrived at Gatwick in the early hours of the morning, we were met by a family friend, a student nurse also from Sierra Leone. She and her boyfriend drove us home. There was nobody there to meet the girl who had been on her own and so we took her with us and slept head to toe, three girls and the student nurse, in the same bed. The next day the girl set off, assuring us she could find her way home. And so we said goodbye.

Later, when I was alone, but old enough to no longer be under the continuous protection of the airline staff, I took a flight to New Zealand to stay with my mother and her husband, my stepfather and a native of that country. The flight was delayed due to snow in London, and when the time did come for us to take off, the pilot announced that we were going to take off on half a runway, that anyone who didn't wish to fly that day was free to disembark. I don't know why I thought he meant a runway of half the width as opposed to half the length, but it wouldn't have changed my decision. The plane raced to the end of the truncated runway and launched into the air, where it failed to make the requisite height and so the pilot flew out over the channel and jettisoned the fuel.

Now we had only enough fuel to get us to Dublin, where the pilot said we would request permission to land and refuel. As the flight went on, it became evident that we were in the hands of a madman. At one point the pilot invited us to look out of the windows on the left-hand side of the craft from where we could see the wreckage of an airliner that had gone down some weeks or months before. I don't remember, or perhaps I never knew which continent we were overflying, which carrier the plane had belonged to or how long the wreckage had lain there. I only recall a snowscape and the stakes that marked out the length and width of the crash site, and which made a giant cross in the snow.

We landed eventually at LAX, but by now I had missed my onward flight. We, the passengers, were bussed to a hotel where we were to spend the night. I was maybe fifteen and alone in Los Angeles. On the bus, a middle-aged British woman with dyed blonde hair worn in stiff, now-tired curls, and who was travelling with her husband, looked over at me and eventually asked if I was alone. 'Stay close to us, love,' she said. And so I tagged along, ending up in the hotel bar with a group of other British travellers where everyone discussed the curious behaviour of the pilot, and where the woman with the curls provoked a small row when she bought me my first gin and tonic. The next day, one of the group, a Cambridge professor of art history, took me to see an exhibition of German expressionism at the Los Angeles Museum of Modern Art, and sometime late in the evening, I caught my plane to Auckland.

In those days I believed in my own immortality, my own inviolability, as only the very young do. In all this time of taking flights alone across the world, I had never been frightened, not even faintly nervous. My fearlessness was also due to all of these events occurring in that fifth dimension of air travel. Here the normal modes of human behaviour do not apply, and we travellers are compatriots of one country. The minor resentments we accrue against other people down on Earth are suspended. There are no ordinary dangers, only extraordinary ones, like crashes and hijacking. This is why flights are, or at least were, so often the setting for movies. In an aeroplane, the passengers are joined in a shared endeavour, which in real life is as simple as arriving at their destination, and in movies may involve delivering babies or taking over the controls after the pilot and co-pilot die. It's hard to be a bystander on a plane—you are automatically involved in whatever happens. All this disappears at the moment of touchdown, and there we are shouldering our way to the exits, all loyalty left in the overhead locker.

Remember back when people used to 'go for a drive' just for the pleasure of the speed and the scenery? Remember when you used to dress up to take a flight? In my family we used to plan our outfits for days in advance and then endure an eight-hour flight in what pretty much constituted a party outfit. Back then you could even smoke. Today there's airport security, rip-off restaurants in the terminals, a lack of legroom inversely proportional to the hours of boredom, the whole process enlivened only by the thought of the drinks trolley and the dinner tray (on airlines where they still serve meals). Chicken or beef? Chicken or beef? Most passengers are so desperate that they're practically thumping out the rhythm on the arm of their seats. And yet, to think only of the tedium is to forget the marvel that is flying.

On an overcast day the plane breaks through the cloud and into sunlight. As the plane climbs, below you clouds shift on separate strata, drifting continents, composed of shadows and light. Sunlight reflects from their dazzling peaks, improbable mountains rise, one the shape perhaps of an anvil or an oak. The occasional sight of another plane reveals the scale of the cloudscape; in it a jumbo jet is reduced to the size of a child's toy as it seems to skate sideways across the sky, its contrail a disappearing scar. There are times when the plane flies between two strata of cloud. Sometimes a hole in the clouds above lets the sunlight through; the rays, edged in darkness, seem to radiate outwards from behind the clouds and illuminate spectacularly, not the earth but the clouds below. We call this God light.

To overfly the Sahara by day at thirty thousand feet is to feel how it might be to circumnavigate the sun. Nothing save raw light in colours from deep orange to pale yellow, very occasionally fractured by imprecise dark and jagged streaks, which one supposes to be riverbeds or rock formations. Otherwise there is but the brightness of the sand reflecting the sun's rays and, depending on the exact altitude and tilt of the aircraft, the line where the orange glow of the ground beneath diffuses into the white band of the horizon, which in turn diffuses into blue sky.

To overfly the Sahara by night must be what space travel feels like. Gone are the indicators of life, the lights of civilisation one sees flying out over what one supposes to be the most barren of lands, even there in some crease in the earth inevitably a winking light or a lone road, leading from where to where it is impossible to know. The Sahara at night is blackness, unmarred by a single star. You cannot tell where the land and sky meet. Only there is this: beyond the reach of the wingtip, a keen-edged moon.

The last time I took a daytime flight over the Sahara was a few years ago on a return trip from Johannesburg. The moment we took off, the cabin staff toured the cabin and lowered the blinds. People found their headsets and turned on the screens in front of them. Light flared around the edges of the blinds and once, when I dared to raise mine over the Sahara, the light leapt in like a living creature. When I fly, I think of what a caveman would think if he saw this, or even knew that one day somebody would. I think of the generations in the not-so-distant past who never saw such a view. I think of those in the future who never will see that wonder which our generation's wantonness with the world's natural resources has made possible. The day will come when we will be nostalgic about flying. As incredible as that once seemed, the experience of having our travel curtailed by the pandemic of 2020 brought that feeling closer to many of us. One day this may be gone, sooner than we allowed ourselves to imagine.

Only in flight does one become aware of how much of the world has resisted humankind. The snow-filled corrugations of the mountain ranges of Central Europe, where it is impossible to know where one country ends and another begins. At such times, even the flight map which traces the path of the plane on the screen in front of you is as effective as pin the tail on the donkey. A ruffle of mountains falls, a new one rises. Once I imagined we must be flying over the Alps, though I think now it was the Massif Central, because a short time later, I looked down and saw the real Alps. I was entirely unprepared for their scale—they seemed to stretch upwards reaching not so much for the sky but as if to swat the plane out of it. I have skied on the Alps and I remember being awed by their beauty, but I could see only what filled the frame of my vision, which I realised, once I was flying over all 1,200 kilometres of them lying across eight countries, wasn't very much at all.

From the window seat, landscapes can seem vast or miniature. Many years ago, my husband took a photograph of a sheer rock face illuminated by an evening light, hues of deep pink, grey and blue. Visitors to our home would stand before it and ask where the formation stood and consider how the picture might have been taken from a low-flying plane, perhaps. My husband would leave them at this for a few minutes and then tell them that the rock formation stood perhaps twenty inches high. On my last trip West out towards El Paso from Washington, DC, I passed over mountainsides the colour of the desert, which bore indentations like those a child makes in a sandpit with a shell or perhaps a fistful of knuckles. There was a dry basin the shape of an open mouth, and beyond that, at the base of a second mountain range, a settlement of houses like dots, which spoke of the mountains' scale. I had an image of a group of settlers, having crossed one mountain range only to be faced by another, giving up and choosing to stay put.

At times like those, one is reminded of man's tenacity, that winking light, a sharp glint where human habitation seems impossible, that lone road, the curl of smoke arising from the mangrove forest. Occasionally, I catch sight of a single vehicle travelling one of those isolated roads. I track the vehicle's passage, wondering if the person inside can sense my gaze, trying to imagine myself in their place and they in mine. In London, where ten million people live, our house lies below the flight path for Heathrow Airport. Once, not the only time

I have done this, I tried to find our street among the rows of terraces in the south-east of the city. I found the spires of Crystal Palace, then Nunhead Cemetery, where I walked the dog most days. I traced the streets: the railway line, Telegraph Hill Park. I craned my neck as we passed over, figured out which street must be ours. Minutes after we landed, I called home. 'Would you reckon you flew over about twenty minutes ago?' my husband asked. That seemed likely. He had been in the garden with our young son, he said, when a plane went over with British Airways written on the underside. He had looked up and said: 'Look, that's Mummy's plane.' And they had waved.

To fly over England, indeed much of northern Europe, is to see a land given over almost entirely to human use, field abuts field, the evidence of human industry. Before views like that, man appears more ant than ape. For a long time, I wondered at the circles that appeared across the American landscape, in different hues and shades from earth to green. Sometimes they appear in ones and twos within an otherwise empty landscape. Other times they arrive in their dozens, in different sizes, overlapping each other, like a Kandinsky painting. Other times still, you see them arranged in rows with architectural precision. They remind me of the crop circles that appear every year in fields in England and which many believe are the result of paranormal activity and others take to be the work of talented pranksters. The American circles are created by central pivot irrigation systems, I discovered when I eventually got around to looking it up. I regretted the sense of intellectual obligation that had propelled me towards this discovery. I liked, I realised, not knowing, gazing at them anew every time. I was interested, though, to see from photographs how the circles, so mystical from the air, were indiscernible on the ground.

Probably, if you have flown across borders very much at all, you will have flown over a war. I know I have. Consider the matter: people are killing and being killed and living in terror of being killed while, at a point precisely overhead, you are doing what? You are watching the drinks trolley edge down the aisle, handling the frustrations of plastic cutlery and those fiddly salt and pepper packets, selecting the next movie, whether it should be a thriller, a drama, a love or a war story. It's likely commercial flights to the country have already stopped, the airport is closed or under the control of one faction or another, the borders will be tightly controlled too. Imagine a person looking up and seeing an aeroplane in the sky, the freedom the passing plane must surely represent. It must be like standing on a desert island, watching the ships pass by, without the possibility even of being able to lift a hand and wave or to shout and be heard.

When I was in my mid-twenties and still immortal, I took the controls of a light aircraft and looped the loop three times. It remains one of the best things I have ever done. My first loop was imperfect. I was so excited, I barely heard the crashing while we were upside down, which was the sound of every loose object falling from its place. I also did not compute the sudden silence as we glided onward. I had taken the plane out of zero gravity and stalled the engine. Paul, my friend, mentioned this as if in passing. I said: 'So now we're flying without an engine?' The plane appeared to have lost no height; we were not spiralling earthward. He leant forward and turned the ignition. I said: 'Can I have another go?'

We had spent the last forty minutes performing aerobatic manoeuvres. We had flown figures of eight and barrel-rolled and dived. We had looped the loop both ways, inside and out. Below me I could see the mouth of the Orwell River and the Orwell Bridge which we had driven across the day before. My only job as passenger was to enjoy the ride and to act as lookout. Look right, look left. Look up, look down. Are there any other planes? No. Spin, climb, dive, roll! It was as simple as that. After a while though, I started feeling queasy. I tried looking at the horizon, but it was never in the same place. Paul said he would take me back, but I wasn't ready for that. So he offered me the controls because the pilot never gets airsick.

To loop the loop you must first get the plane up to a certain speed, around 140 mph, keeping the wings perfectly level. Find something to line the nose of the aircraft up to, that will help you navigate. I used the Orwell Bridge. Then you pull the joystick firmly but slowly towards your belly. The nose of the aircraft starts to rise, as the plane begins the first 180-degree turn. It feels like taking a heavy car up a too-steep hill; at any moment you might begin to slide backwards. You're pressed into your seat by the force. Now you're upside down and, this is the tricky bit, you need to ease off the stick so the plane floats over the arc of the loop before you begin the return journey, at which point you begin to push the joystick away. The second time I looped the loop I made the same mistake as the first. Well, it was so very hard to keep it all going upside down, to keep looking and thinking and doing. The third time, which was to be the last because Paul thought people watching from the clubhouse might start to ask why he was flying so amateurishly, I executed my loop proficiently. Every item in the cockpit, including the packet of Marlboros on the

dash, stayed in its place for the entire 360-degree rotation. I
flew out of the loop, my wings level, feeling like the gymnast
who has just dismounted the beam having scored a perfect
ten as I zoomed into the blue yonder.

As I say, in those days I was immortal. Mortality, though,
was only a decade away. In my mid-thirties I went through
a period of being nervous of flying. I know people who must
take a sedative or be blind drunk before they fly. I had none
of that. Instead, I suffered sweaty palms every time the plane
lurched through a patch of turbulence. I would eye the cabin
staff for evidence of an emergency, already knowing they are
trained to act like automatons even as the pilot loses control
and the plane goes down. Some years back my husband's
cousin flew first class to Los Angeles. What made this possible was the fact that his wife was an attendant working the
same flight: they were on the start of their honeymoon. After
they landed, he looked out of the window to find the plane
surrounded by emergency vehicles. Sometime into the flight,
someone had written a bomb threat upon a mirror in one of
the bathrooms. His wife never told him. That's how good
they are.

One often hears that statistically a fear of flying is irratio-
nal. But to me the fear of flying is entirely rational, a response
to the absurdity of what we are doing—flying in a pressurised
metal tube, thousands of feet up, breathing recycled air. Our
chances of crashing may be considerably lower than travelling
in a car, but that's not what people who are afraid of flying
are thinking about; rather they're figuring their chances of
survival if the worst happens. Maybe it's the knowledge of
Icarus's folly that makes passengers lower the blind, turn on
the screen, and put on the earphones to escape into irreality.

Once, in the Gambia, in 2000, I boarded a flight I began to have serious doubts would make it. I was trying to get to my family in Freetown at a time when commercial airlines had stopped flying there, as they did during the civil war and would again fourteen years later as Ebola gripped the country. I wrote about my return to Sierra Leone and that flight at the time:

> From the outside the West Coast Airlines aircraft looked respectable enough; inside it was another matter entirely. The seats were tattered and stained, many of the seatbelts were broken, the overhead lockers were wooden and refused to open; instead our hand baggage was taken from us and thrown into a void in the tail of the aircraft.
>
> As we waited in our seats before take-off I watched the two Russian pilots making their way to the cockpit. I wondered, briefly, what in the world could have brought these two men to be here, commandeering an ageing aircraft in and out of unstable African states.

What I didn't include, because it happened three years later, was that the same aircraft, on its way from Freetown to Beirut, went down with the loss of one hundred and forty souls. I was in Freetown at the time, the war had been over by a year, it was the day after Christmas. Everywhere I went there was someone who knew someone on that flight. We were all just one degree of separation from tragedy.

Somehow that experience brought me, rather than a heightened sense of panic, a renewed calm about flying. I stopped worrying about what I could not control. Now it becomes a moment to make peace with the possibility of death. I think about the things that I have done and those I have left undone. (I always feel just a tad more relaxed when a book I have been writing is finished.) I think about those people I love and have loved. I consider the movie programming and discard it. I fold my hands in my lap, lean back and turn my head to the window and wait for the force that pushes me back into my seat.

Ice

When I go to the theatre, I like to sit a good way back from the stage. There is no mystery to this. I'm afraid the moment might come when an actor steps down from the stage and chooses me, me—out of all the upturned faces of the members of the audiences—to go on stage. This last happened on my first date with the man who is now my husband. The theatre was tiny, probably seating no more than thirty. The distance from our seats to the stage was perilously short. A performer who looked and danced like a budget Leo Sayer pulled me from my seat and made me dance on stage. I'm the kind of person this happens to a lot. Perhaps because in many of the places I have lived I tend to stand out. Also, I do not have resting bitch face. Instead I have the sort of face that makes people think I am kindlier than I am. So, like the career criminal who never sits with his back to the door, I avoid the seats near the stage. Nobody enjoys the humiliation of a forced public performance, but my fear runs deeper than that and the psychological trajectory, for once, is a straight line.

In 1970, newly arrived in London, my stepmother thought it would be a fine idea to take us all to a show, my sister,

brother and I. The production was *Disney on Ice* at Wembley
Stadium. The arena sits twelve and a half thousand people.
Our finances at that time were a little thin, so this was a special
Christmastime treat. We were seated in the front row which
afforded an excellent view of the ice. We had chocolates and
fizzy drinks, all of which added to our state of excitement.
Our seats were at the end of the row—my stepmother took
the place closest to the aisle, I sat next to her, because at six I
was the youngest, then came my sister and finally my brother,
the eldest. For the ice spectacle the entire floor of the arena was
converted into a magnificent rink. Being, at that time, a child
of Africa, I had never seen real skaters; probably I was only
peripherally aware that such an activity existed from reading
the kinds of Victorian children's stories available at the British
Council Library in Freetown. In no way could my imagination
have prepared me for such a sight—all the characters from my
favourite films right there in front of me, gliding forwards and
backwards, they spun, pirouetted and leaped, moved by some
invisible propulsion. There was music of course, and probably
some attempt at a narrative; I don't remember anything about
that. This is what I do remember: Snow White leading the
Seven Dwarves in a conga line; Dumbo, flat on his belly, legs
to the four directions of the wind, rotating slowly centre ice.
How we laughed! And then, to the sound of the 'Bare Necessi-
ties,' led by Mowgli himself, joined by Bagheera, Shere Khan,
King Louie, Colonel Hathi and Baloo. Gentle, dumb but not
so dumb Baloo, my favourite. Baloo patted his stomach and
dipped his head in that 'Aw shucks' way he had. He stumbled,
pretended to trip and righted himself as Mowgli chased him
around the ice. Baloo was the star of my show.

Suddenly the performers split up and began skating in multiple directions. They were coming *off the ice*! And they no longer glided but walked with an odd, clunky gait, hobbled by their skates. They were taking children from their seats, one by one, lifting them up and carrying them off. And then there was Baloo. He reached past my stepmother and snatched me from my seat. Baloo up close was not the Baloo of the *Jungle Book* film or even Baloo of the ice. This Baloo had a face made of plastic, and hard plastic paws. And his eyes were not soft, brown, bear eyes. Through the cut-out holes of the mask, I could see the small, blue eyes of a man. I cried out. I wriggled. And I fought. But Baloo was strong, Baloo held on tight. And then we were on the ice, speeding away from everything I knew. The audience clapped and cheered. 'Take me back,' I cried. And Baloo, my once beautiful Baloo, dug his fingers and thumbs hard into my body, leaned forward and hissed with hot breath into my ear: 'Shut up, you little shit!'

Obama and the
Renaissance Generation

It came to be a core belief held by the American public and media that Barack Obama was a self-creation who had seemingly stepped out of nowhere. In a racially divided society, for some voters the idea that he held no tribal affiliation was part of his attraction. For his detractors, of whom Trump and his Birther Movement were the most visible, the same belief provided an opportunity to claim that Obama was not a true American. Obama did indeed cut a solitary figure: parents and American grandparents dead, no full siblings; what else there was of his family lived in Kenya, which might as well have been the moon to many Americans. Marriage to Michelle gave Obama what he appeared to lack: a family and a community. His Kenyan ancestry, though, meant that Obama joined the African American community by adoption rather than birthright.

Against the backdrop of the fantasy of normality which much American popular culture promotes—that all but a few people live in the same place all their lives—Obama's story appeared unusual. The truth is that his grandparents made the move to Hawaii (after several around the country), doing what millions of Americans do and have always done: searching for better opportunities. One result is that families become stretched over distance and time until the links between uncles, aunts, cousins and generations are broken and reformed with new generations in new places.

Even so, the standout fact of Obama's biography remained and remains that he had been born of a Kenyan father and a white mother. 'No life could have been more the product of randomness than that of Barack Obama,' wrote David Maraniss in his 2012 biography of the former president. This, though, is the case only when his life is viewed from an American perspective. From an African perspective, the tradition of sending young men to study overseas, as was the case with Barack Obama Sr, is a familiar and long-standing one. In 1852, William Wells Brown, the American playwright, fugitive slave, and abolitionist, noted that he might meet half a dozen black students in an hour's walk through central London. Some sixty years before that, in 1791, the Temne king Naimbana (of what became Sierra Leone in West Africa) sent his son John Frederick to England, for reasons of political expediency (he sent another to France, and a third to North Africa to acquire an Islamic education). Tragically, John Frederick never made it home but died on the return passage.

In the second half of the twentieth century, geopolitical events—the end of empires, the rise of nationalism in African countries, the Cold War, communism and the second 'Red Scare'—would see an exponential rise in the number of Africans sent to study overseas. So the meeting of Obama's parents came about more as the unintended consequence of political policy than by random chance. For me, Obama's story is remarkably familiar. My parents met under very similar circumstances. My father was born in 1935 in Sierra Leone; Barack Obama Sr was born in Kenya in 1936. My mother was white and British; Obama's mother was a white American. Both women met and married the men who would become our respective fathers when those men were selected to study at university abroad—a story Obama relates only briefly in his memoir *Dreams from My Father*:

> My father grew up herding his father's goats and attending the local school, set up by the British colonial administration, where he had shown great promise. He eventually won a scholarship to study in Nairobi; and then on the eve of Kenyan independence, he had been selected by Kenyan leaders and American sponsors to attend a university in the United States, joining the first wave of Africans to be sent forth to master Western technology and bring it back to forge a new, modern Africa.

Obama was wrong about one thing: his father was not
in the first wave of students sent overseas to master Western
technology, though he was in the first wave of *Kenyans* who
were sent to *America*. Up until then, most African students
had been destined for Britain and, starting after the Second
World War, to the Soviet Bloc and China. In fact, the adventures of this generation of Africans would one day inspire a
genre of literature, collectively known as the "been to" novels,
exemplified by Ayi Kwei Armah's *Fragments*, *No Longer at
Ease* by Chinua Achebe, and Ama Ata Aidoo's *Dilemma of a
Ghost*, fictions that told of the challenges both of leaving the
motherland for the West and of return.

My father's story was both extraordinary and yet, in its own
way, entirely typical of the changing times in which he was
born. The son of a wealthy farmer and a regent chief from the
north of Sierra Leone, Mohamed Forna had won a scholarship at an early age to the elite Bo School, many miles from
home in the south of the country. At the time, Sierra Leone
was a British colony, though one that was never settled by
whites, who, unable to tolerate the climate, died in such
droves from malaria and tropical illnesses that the country
was dubbed 'the white man's grave.' British fragility made
a crucial difference to the style of governance Britain chose
to adopt in West Africa. Instead of a full-fledged colonial
government such as existed in Kenya, where the climate of
the Highlands was suited to both coffee and Europeans, in
Sierra Leone the guardians of Empire relied instead on a
system of 'native administration.' Bo School was founded
by the British for the sons of the local aristocracy, who,

according to plan, would play a leading role in governing Sierra Leone on behalf of the British.

Generally, the British were cautious about allowing their colonial subjects much in the way of book learning. The colonial project had begun with a great deal of hubris, talk of a civilising mission and the belief that Britain could create the world in its own image. Education was a part of that mission. But by the time Lord Lugard, the colonial administrator and architect of native administration, became the governor of Nigeria in 1912, he was sounding warnings against 'the Indian disease,' namely the creation, through education, of an intellectual class who would go on to embrace nationalism. Burned by the threat of insurrection elsewhere in the Empire, though still intent on the pursuit of an administration staffed by local talent, the British allowed a few Africans just enough education to create a core of black bureaucrats, but no more.

Sierra Leone's beginnings were a little different from those of Britain's other African holdings. In the late eighteenth century, British philanthropists had established settlements there of people freed from slavery, many of whom had fled from America to Britain following Lord Mansfield's 1772 ruling that protected escaped slaves. As part of this social engineering experiment, schools and even a university were established in the capital, Freetown. Fourah Bay College, founded in 1827, was the first institute of higher education built in West Africa since the demise of the Islamic universities in Timbuktu. Elsewhere in Britain's African dominions, and in the early days of Empire, most educational establishments were built by evangelically motivated Christian missionaries, and they were tolerated but not encouraged by the colonial administration.

In Kenya, in the 1920s, precisely what Lugard feared began to happen: missionary-educated Kenyan men established their own churches and challenged white rule. The locals had a name for Western-educated Kenyans: Asomi. Harry Thuku, the Father of Kenyan Nationalism (whose story is narrated in Ngũgĩ wa Thiong'o's tale of the Mau Mau Rebellion, *A Grain of Wheat*), was one such man. In their churches, Asomi pastors accused the missionaries of distorting the Bible's message to their own ends and preached an Africanised version of Christianity, and the Asomi founded associations to represent African interests and built their own schools in which pupils were imbued with a sense of patriotism and pride.

Still, whatever resistance Britain's Colonial Office offered to the idea of the educated native, by the later days of Empire, faced with ever-growing demands for colonial reform, the British began to build a limited number of government institutions, with the intention, in the words of the Conservative minister Oliver Stanley in 1943, of guiding 'Colonial people along the road to self-government within the framework of the British Empire.' Any future form of self-governance was intended to create the basis for neocolonialism and a bulwark against the threat of communism.

Shifts in British attitudes, however, were soon outstripped by African ambitions. One million African men had fought on the Allied side during the Second World War, and those experiences had broadened their worldview. Many had learned to read and write—among them, Obama's grandfather, Onyango, who, according to Obama family lore, travelled to Burma, Ceylon, the Middle East and Europe as a British officer's cook. Whether Onyango knew how to read and write English before he was recruited is unknown; it is possible, though unlikely. By the time he came back, however, he was able to teach his young son his letters before sending him to school. In *Dreams from My Father*, Barack Obama recounts Onyango's surviving sister's and his great aunt Dorsila's memories of his grandfather: 'To [Onyango] knowledge was the source of all the white man's power, and he wanted to make sure his son was as educated as any white man.'

Across the continent, emerging nationalist movements were gaining ground. For them, literacy, followed by the creation of an elite class of professionals, were the necessary first steps toward full independence. The courses on offer at the government colleges were restricted in subject and scope (syllabuses had to be approved by the colonial authorities) and the colleges themselves could admit only a limited number of students. Energised and impatient, a new generation refused to wait or to play by the Englishman's rules. With too few opportunities on the continent, they set their sights overseas, on Britain itself.

Few had the means to cover the costs of travel and fees. There were a limited number of scholarships available through the colonial governments, mainly to study subjects the local universities were not equipped to teach, such as medicine. A lucky few found wealthy patrons; others still were sponsored by donations from their extended families, and sometimes from entire villages. The Ghanaian nationalist and politician Joe Appiah, father of the philosopher Kwame Anthony Appiah, ditched his job in Freetown without telling his employers and bought himself a one-way ticket on a ship bound for Liverpool, hoping to get by on his luck and wit.

My mother, Maureen, has a particular memory of my father. On April 27, 1961, the day Sierra Leone became a self-governing nation, he got roaring drunk at a sherry party held by African students on the premises of the British Council in Aberdeen. The couple had married at the registry office in Aberdeen one month before, in a ceremony attended by their friends among the West African students.

On the way home, on the top deck of the bus, my father lit six cigarettes and puffed on them all at once. 'But, Mohamed, you don't even smoke,' my mother had protested. And my father replied: 'I'm smoking the smoke of freedom, man. I'm smoking the smoke of freedom.'

In the decades between the two world wars, Britain emerged as 'the locus of resistance to empire' where anti-colonial movements were shaped by the growth of Pan-Africanist ideals among artists, intellectuals, students and activists from the colonies. Ngũgĩ wa' Thiong'o, commenting on his arrival in Leeds in 1964, once remarked to me:

> For the first time I was able to look back at Kenya and Africa, from outside Kenya. Many of the things that were happening in Africa at that time, independence and all that, were not clear to me when I was in Kenya but made sense when I was in Leeds meeting other students from Africa, Nigeria, Ghana, students from Australia, every part of the Commonwealth, students from Bulgaria, Greece, Iraq, Afghanistan—we all met there in Leeds, we had encounters with Marx with Lenin, and all that began to clarify for me a change of perspective.

Among those elites who gathered there, driven by, and driving, the desire for self-rule, were Jomo Kenyatta, the first president of Kenya; Kwame Nkrumah, the first president of Ghana; Michael Manley, three-term prime minister of Jamaica; Marcus Garvey, a founder of the American Black nationalist movement; the writer and activist CLR James; Seretse Khama, first president of Botswana; Julius Nyerere, first president of Tanzania. Also, a number of African Americans, including the singer, actor and activist Paul Robeson and his wife, the anthropologist Eslanda Goode Robeson. In London, anti-colonial and Pan-Africanist ideas were shared and enlarged, spurred by a shared experience as colonial subjects in their homelands and as the victims of racism and the colour bar in Britain. 'They were brought together too by the fact that the British—those who helped and those who hindered—saw them all as Africans, first of all,' writes Anthony Appiah. And so those who may previously never have identified themselves as such began to do so and explore the commonalities of race, racism and nationalism. And out of those conversations arose new political possibilities involving international organisations and the opportunity for cultural exchange.

Arrival in Britain brought with it many shocks for the colonial student. Whereas before they were Sierra Leonian and Temne, Luo and Kenyan, Hausa and Nigerian, suddenly they were simply black, subject to all the attitudes and reactions conferred by their skin colour. Landlords often refused to rent their properties to black tenants during my father's time in Scotland. My mother told me of the insults my father endured in the street—directed at her as well, when they were together. Later, my father's second wife, Yabome—my stepmother, who also went to university in Aberdeen and vacationed in London, staying in the apartments of other African students—recalled the gangs of racist skinheads who arrived to break up their gatherings. 'Somebody would run and call for the West

Indians,' she told me, their Caribbean neighbours being more experienced in fending off such attacks. In a reversal of the immigrant dream story, Sam Selvon's 1956 novel *The Lonely Londoners* tells the tale of black people arriving in the 1950s in search of prosperity and a new life, only to discover cruelty and misery.

In order to confront the challenges of their new lives, as well as to keep abreast of political developments back home, the colonial students organised themselves into societies and associations. One such was the hugely influential West African Students' Union, or WASU. If London was the heart of resistance, then WASU was its circulatory system. My father and his friends were all WASU members, as was every former West African student of that time to whom I have ever spoken. WASU was the centre of their social, cultural and, especially, political life. It also 'functioned as a training ground for leaders of the West African nationalist movement,' wrote the historian Peter Fryer; indeed, both Kwame Nkrumah and Joe Appiah were among the leading names who served on WASU's executive committee.

Unnerved at the pace with which calls for independence were gathering, the Colonial Office kept a close eye on the students' activities. In London, the department funded two hostels, which aided the many whom the colour bar prevented from finding decent lodging (and also kept them conveniently in one location). The civil servants also spied on the African students through MI5. A tug-of-war was taking place within the Colonial Office: on one side were the 'softly softlies' who favoured an approach designed to promote good relations with the future leaders; on the other were the hardliners who were concerned that Communist ideas might take root among the rising generation. Such was the fear of Communist-inspired insurrection in West Africa that Marxist literature was banned and travel to Eastern European countries was restricted in countries under British rule.

The colonial administrator Lord Milverton once described WASU as 'a communist medium for the contact of communists with West Africans' through the Communist Party of Great Britain. Then parliamentarian David Rees Williams even accused the Communist Party of using prostitutes to spread its message and called for restrictions on the numbers of students entering the country from the colonies. Though MI5 did not go so far as to keep individual files on all the students, it did do so for the most visible leaders like Nkrumah, whose phone it tapped.

Certainly, there were Marxist sympathisers among the WASU leadership and the African student body in general. Ngũgĩ wa' Thiong'o talked to me about his road to Marxism, which began during his student years in Leeds, when he saw poor whites for the first time and witnessed, during the student demonstrations in Leeds, white policemen turning on their own, a 'vicious crushing of dissent.' Julius Nyerere turned to socialism during his time in Edinburgh, returning to Tanzania in 1952 to become a union organiser and later the first president of a new, socialist republic.

By the 1960s, with the colonies gaining independence one by one, and China and the Soviet bloc beginning to offer their own scholarships, the softly softly approach had prevailed within Britain's Colonial Office. The administration of the students' affairs was handed over to the British Council, which began a diplomatic charm offensive. Before they even left home, students on government scholarships

were offered induction seminars on what to wear and how
to conduct themselves in the homes of British people and
shown films on how to navigate the challenges of daily life.
In one of these films, entitled *Lost in the Countryside*, a pair of
Africans abroad (dressed in tweeds, they emerge from behind
a haystack) are instructed firmly: 'Do not panic! Find a road.
Locate a bus stop. Join the queue [and there in the middle of
nowhere is a line of people]. A bus will arrive. Board it and
return to town.' Once the students were in the UK, the British
Council arranged homestays for those Africans who wanted
an up-close experience of the British (some 9,500 said they
did). My stepmother, Yabome, recalls being advised never to
sit in the chair of the head of household, a faux pas of which
she has retained a dread all her life.

And finally, there were social events at the Council's premises in various British cities. At a Christmas dance in the
winter of 1959, my father, a third-year medical student at
Aberdeen University, approached a young woman, a volunteer
named Maureen who was helping to pour drinks for the party,
put out his hand and said: 'I'm Mohamed.'

If the attitude of the British authorities toward the West Africans was one of wavering welcome, the attitude toward the
East Africans, Kenyans in particular, was even more complicated. In 1945, there were about one thousand colonial students in Britain, two thirds of whom came from West Africa
and only sixty-five of whom came from East Africa. In Kenya,
a simmering mood of rebellion had, by the 1950s, given rise to
the Mau Mau, a movement that explicitly rejected white rule
and gave voice to the resentment against colonial government
taxes, low wages and the miserable living conditions endured

by many Kenyans. The Mau Mau, which found its support mainly among the Kikuyu people who had been displaced from rural areas by white farmers, demanded political representation and the return of their land. Facing armed insurrection, in 1952 the British declared a state of emergency, and tried and imprisoned the nationalist leader (who would later become the first president of Kenya) Jomo Kenyatta, who had returned to his homeland from London in 1947.

Upon Kenyatta's imprisonment, Kenyan nationalists turned to the United States for help. The activist Tom Mboya, a rising political star who in 1960 featured on *Time* magazine's cover as the face of the new Africa, became the strongest voice calling for independence in Kenyatta's absence. In 1959, Mboya began working with African American organisations—in particular, the historically Black private and state colleges, as well as civil rights champions such as Harry Belafonte, Sidney Poitier, Jackie Robinson and Martin Luther King Jr—and toured the United States talking about Black civil rights and African nationalism as two sides of the same coin. His aim was to raise money for a scholarship program to bring Kenyan students to the US. Over two months, Mboya gave a hundred speeches and met with then vice president Richard Nixon at the White House. By that point, independence for Kenya was a matter of when, not if—after all, Ghana had already attained independence—and it looked very much as though Britain was deliberately refusing Kenyans the help they needed to prepare for self-governance.

So here was Mboya offering the United States a foothold of influence in Africa, which Britain, even against the backdrop of a Cold War scramble for the allegiance of African nations, was too churlish or too arrogant to secure. Although Nixon stopped short of agreeing to meet Mboya's request for help, the Democratic candidate for the 1960 presidential election, John F. Kennedy, did do so and his family's foundation donated $100,000 (the equivalent of nearly one million dollars today) to what became known as the 'African student airlifts,' the first of which had taken place in 1957.

Mboya was a member of the Luo people, a friend of Onyanga's, and sometime mentor to his son, Barack Obama Sr. On his own initiative, Obama Sr had managed to secure himself an offer from the University of Hawaii, and this won him a place on a later airlift in 1959. Here was a young man with an excellent brain, and here, too, was a new dawn on the horizon bringing with it a new country—Obama Sr saw himself as part of it all. Wole Soyinka, who himself studied at Leeds in the 1950s, would later call his generation the 'Renaissance Generation.'

Just as the West African students bound for Britain had been coached in what to expect, so the Kenyans were briefed on arrival in the United States, including about the prevailing racial attitudes they should expect to encounter there. The world-renowned anthropologist, and now director of the Makerere Institute of Research, Mahmood Mamdani, who travelled to the US on a 1963 Kenyan airlift, recalls being told it would be 'preferable for us to wear African clothing when going into the surrounding communities because then people would know we were African and we would be dealt with respectfully.' Under colonial rule, Kenyans certainly did not share the privileges of whites; even so, for many African students the daily indignities of racial segregation in America came as a shock. At least one was arrested for trying to buy a sandwich at a whites-only lunch counter, and some of those studying at universities in the South were prompted by their experience of Southern racism to ask to be transferred to Northern colleges. As had been the case for their counterparts in Britain, a close eye was kept on their activities. Returning from a trip to Montgomery, Alabama, Mamdani got a visit from FBI agents; he recalls that they asked if he liked Marx, to which Mamdani replied in perfect innocence that he had never met the man. Informed that Marx was dead, he replied: 'Oh no! What happened?' And as he told me in our conversation many years later: 'The abiding outcome of that visit was that I went to the library to look up Marx.'

Obama Sr's choice of the University of Hawaii was, in many ways, an unfortunate one. Hawaii was more cosmopolitan than other parts of the United States and he did at least escape some of the racist attitudes that confronted other African students, but he was far from all the debates, meetings, lobbying and activism about independence that were taking place at the universities and historically Black colleges on the mainland. When the opportunity arose, he chose to continue his studies at Harvard, and part of the reason was undoubtedly that he wanted to get closer to the action. In 1961, Kenyatta was released from jail; two years later, Kenya declared independence. When all that happened, Obama was still a long way from home—just as my father was when Sierra Leone won its independence.

In time, Ngũgĩ would return from Leeds, and Mamdani from the United States. Ngũgĩ was by then a published author, having abandoned his studies to write *Weep Not, Child,* a tale of dispossession and resistance set during the Mau Mau Rebellion. Mamdani went on to teach at Makerere University, which became the venue for the famous 1962

African Writers' Conference, where a generation of the continent's most promising young writers, including Ngũgĩ, met to debate and define the future of African literature. Later Mamdani helped to transform the school from a colonial technical college into a vibrant university. One of the few women on the airlift, Wangari Maathai flew back home from Pittsburgh in 1966, later to found the Green Belt Movement, an initiative focusing on environmental conservation that today is credited with planting fifty-one million trees in Kenya and for which Maathai would be awarded a Nobel Peace Prize. Still, for Kenya, as for every one of the new African nations, independence proved a steep and rocky road. Five hundred students who had earned their degrees overseas returned home, a significant proportion of them the American-educated Asomi. They would become the educators, administrators, accountants, lawyers, doctors, judges and businessmen in the new Kenya. Despite the best efforts of Tom Mboya and his supporters, Kenya had only a fraction of the college-educated young professionals it needed.

Eight years after he had left Sierra Leone, my father returned. His elder brother had died, and his family wrote that Mohamed was needed at home. By then, he was a qualified medical doctor, with a wife and three children. The year before, Obama Sr had also returned home after the US government declined to renew his visa. Medical students and those who went on to higher degrees, especially, had found themselves away for long periods, as much as a decade. Unsurprisingly, in that time, many of the men had formed romantic attachments with local women. If those relationships were frowned upon in Britain, they were illegal in much of America. *Loving* v. *Virginia*, the case before the Supreme Court that finally overturned the ban on interracial unions, was not decided until 1967. When the Immigration and Naturalization Service declined Obama Sr's request to remain in the country, his relations with women were reported to be part of the problem. Already, he had fathered a son with Ann Dunham, Barack Jr, but that marriage was over. Subsequently, he had formed a new relationship with another white woman, Ruth Baker.

In Britain, the authorities, though they did not encourage such unions, did not intervene except, notably, in the case of Seretse Khama, heir to the Bangwato chieftaincy in Bechuanaland (now Botswana), and Ruth Williams. This was at the behest of white-ruled South Africa, whose government would not tolerate an interracial marriage within its borders. Jomo Kenyatta had a child, Peter, with his British wife. I used to pass Peter in the corridors of the BBC, where for a time we both worked; he was in management, while I was a junior reporter awed by the prestige of his last name. The marriage of Anthony Appiah's parents, Joe Appiah and Peggy Cripps, who was the daughter of the Labour politician Sir Stafford Cripps, was one of the most high-profile unions of the day that also happened to be a mixed marriage.

Of Ann Dunham, first wife to Obama Sr and mother of the future president, a childhood friend would later say: 'She just became really, really interested in the world. Not afraid of newness or difference. She was afraid of smallness.' The same could be said of my mother, Maureen Christison. Aberdeen was simply too small for her. The African students represented a world beyond the grey waters of the North Sea. In the Scottish writer Jackie Kay's *Red Dust*, her 2010 memoir of her search for her Nigerian father who studied in Scotland in the 1950s, her father overturns conventional wisdom in remarking how popular the male African students were with the local girls. The men frequently came from aristocratic families—both Appiah and Khama were royal, and my father was the son of a regent chief and landowner. 'You must remember,' a contemporary of my parents observed during the time when I was researching my own memoir of my father, 'they were the chosen ones.'

In 2017, in a *New York Times* op-ed assessing President Obama's foreign policy legacy, Adam Shatz noted that Obama was 'a well-traveled cosmopolitan . . . seemingly at home wherever he planted his feet. His vision of international diplomacy stressed the virtues of candid dialogue, mutual respect and bridge building.' Obama's cosmopolitanism was rooted in several places: the *fact* of his Kenyan father (though not his immediate influence, since Obama Sr was gone from the family before Obama was old enough to remember him), and later his painstaking search to assemble the pieces of his birthright, which would do much to extend his vision. But before all of that, it was his mother, Ann, who instilled in him the foundations of his internationalism. She rehearsed for her son the version of his father's story that Obama Sr told of himself: that of the idealist devoted to building a new Kenya—albeit that in reality he was an unreliable husband and father, whose career came well short of his own expectations. It was Ann who remained true to that vision of a new world, who easily made friends with people of different nationalities, who subsequently married an Indonesian, and took her son to Indonesia to spend a formative period of his childhood, where she spent many years running development projects. My mother, Maureen, never returned to Scotland following the break-up of her marriage to my father. After she got married again, to a New Zealander who worked for the United Nations, she spent her life moving around the world, in time building her own international career within the UN.

Both women entered an international professional class, a group that the British historian David Goodhart disparagingly describes as the 'anywheres': people whose sense of self is not rooted in a single place or readymade local identity. If Obama's search in *Dreams from My Father* was a quest for his African identity, it was also, and conversely, an attempt to discover whether he could ever be a 'somewhere,' whether that somewhere was a place (in time, he would choose Chicago) or a people, part of an African American community.

His next book, *The Audacity of Hope*, became, by contrast, a plea for complexity. Of his extended family of Indonesians, white Americans, Africans and Chinese—in which I find a mirror for mine: African, European, Iranian, New World and Chinese—Obama writes: 'I've never had the option of restricting my loyalties on the basis of race or measuring my worth on the basis of tribe.' Obama knew and understood that he had more than one identity, that all of us do. Anthony Appiah credits his own avowed cosmopolitanism to his father Joe's relaxed way with people from different worlds. I believe my father thought that his children would grow up to be both Sierra Leonian and British, a new kind of citizen, a new African, comfortable with our place in the world.

For all the hope, there were bitter disappointments as well. Shortly after Obama Sr returned to Kenya, his mentor Tom

Mboya was assassinated. Obama Sr would lose himself to drink and die in a car crash. My father arrived back in Sierra Leone to a government openly talking of introducing a one-party system, a threat to his democratic ideals. As politically opportunistic leaders across the continent quickly realised how easily the newborn institutions of democracy could be subverted to personal gain, the returning graduates would find themselves forced to confront the very governments they had come home to serve. In Ghana, Joe Appiah was jailed by his former good friend Nkrumah; Ngũgĩ wa' Thiong'o would be imprisoned for sedition against the Kenyan government and then exiled; in Nigeria, Soyinka encountered a similar fate. My father was jailed and killed. Many would pay a high price for the privilege of having travelled beyond Africa, for coming of age at the same time as their countries, for working and dreaming of a Renaissance yet to come.

How many times in my own travels in this world have I come across one of them, the chosen of my father's generation? There's a quality of character they wear, whose origins I have come to understand. They carry, alongside a worldly ease, a sense of duty, of obligation and responsibility, that imbues all they say and do. Unlike the generations that followed, they never saw their own future beyond Africa. I try to imagine an Africa if they had never been, and I cannot. There are those the world over who decry the failings and weaknesses of the post-independence African states at the same time as many in the West—after Afghanistan, after Iraq, and facing assaults on their own democratic institutions—have slowly come to the realisation that nation-building is no simple task, that democracy takes more than a parliament building. The generation of Africans to whom the task fell of creating new countries knew, or came to know, that alongside the desires and dreams, and the promise of a newfound freedom, they had been set up to fail. Their real courage lay in the fact that they did not surrender, that they tried to do what they had promised themselves and their countries they would. They went forward anyway.

Santigi

Santigi was a foundling. Or at least Santigi was as close to being a foundling as you can imagine. None of us, not even Santigi, knew his origins. He knew the name of the village where he was born but had never been back there. He did not know the names of his mother or his father. He called himself a Loko, for the reason that he understood the language, which was his only tie to his beginnings. 'Santigi, the Loko,' we'd call him, and he would bang himself on the chest and say, 'Loko!'

For Yabome, my stepmother, her first memory of Santigi was when he met her off the train from school. At the time Santigi had come to live in the house with Yabome and the grandmother who raised her. At that age Yabome never thought to ask from where Santigi had come, and when her grandmother died the old lady took whatever knowledge she possessed with her. It was rumoured that Santigi's mother had borne him alone, had left him with neighbours while she went to find work scratching for diamonds in the eastern mines and that she had died there. When she failed to return, the neighbours had given her young son to the old lady to raise. The story makes some kind of sense, but still it is hard to imagine, in a country where kinship is everything, where ties of allegiance are what binds, in a small country where everybody knows everyone else and their business, that a woman could be so alone. As for Santigi, if you asked him, all he ever told you was that he was a Loko. He made Yabome his family. When she returned from Scotland, where she went to college on a scholarship, Santigi was waiting for her. And when she married my father, Santigi came along too.

Nobody knew how old Santigi was. In her first memory of him, of being met by him off the train at Magburaka, home on holiday from Harford School for Girls in Moyamba, my stepmother would have been twelve and guessed him to be a few years older, perhaps sixteen. Yabome's father had been a merchant who traded in gold. Possessed of unusual foresight for the time, he had made sure every one of his children went to school and to university. In those days we had several cousins living with us whose school fees my father paid. Santigi wanted to go to school too, but my father said he was already too old. Instead, he sent Santigi to adult education classes at night. Often, when I came back from school in the afternoon, Santigi would sit next to me at the dining-room table while I did my homework and copy out the questions and answers in his own exercise book.

If life had gone on in that way, maybe Santigi would somehow have realised his dream to go to college, though I don't remember his ambitions being taken particularly seriously. His enthusiasm for learning was not, it seems, matched by aptitude. And even if it were, it would not have helped for all our lives were about to change. By 1970, Sierra Leone was a nascent dictatorship, a one-party state was on the rise. My father was arrested and jailed for his opposition to the prime minister. Our household scattered. The cooks and stewards, the driver—all departed. My cousins went back to live with their families. Mum, my sister and brother and I went into hiding and then into exile in London, where we would stay for three years.

Only Santigi stayed on, living in the empty rooms of our house. He guarded our possessions against thieves and every week he went to the Pademba Road Prison, where my father was being held. He brought my father food and clean clothes and he took away his washing, returning it ironed and folded the following week. In times like those loyalty is hard to find, and Santigi earned our family's loyalty in return for his. But to me, looking back, what he did was more powerful than mere loyalty. Violence was on the rise, our home had been stoned by political thugs, those same thugs raided newspaper offices, threatened journalists, university professors and lawyers, and beat up anyone who dared to oppose the prime minister in his determination to become president-for-life. All our household staff had been held and detained at CID (Criminal Investigation Department) headquarters, my stepmother, too, and Santigi. Santigi had been badly beaten. As he waited at the prison gates, Santigi would have been taunted by the guards, I am sure, as were the prisoners themselves. His visits to my father were an act of loyalty and of courage; they were also an act of resistance. Like the Mothers, now the Grandmothers of the Plaza de Mayo, who come out every day in Buenos Aires to march in memory of their disappeared sons and daughters, so Santigi came every week to the prison gates to remind the authorities that my father was not forgotten. When my father was released—taken to the prison gates and let out without warning—he had no money for a taxi, but a passing driver recognised him and gave him a lift. When he arrived home Santigi was there. It was Santigi who cooked my father's first meal as a free man.

In the year that followed, the pleasure of being reunited, of my father's freedom, made us giddy. We danced to that year's hit 'Kung Fu Fighting,' we sang and we punched and kicked the air. We, the three children and our older cousins: Morlai, Esther, Agnes and, of course, Santigi. Santigi got religion around that time and changed his name to Simon Peter and then to Santos. He carried a Bible around, and he also talked about his dream of becoming a photographer, even though he had never owned a camera. I would, in my university years, buy him a camera and I believe he did, for a while, have a small booth where he took portraits. But all that was some years off. A year after he was freed, my father was arrested again, this time on charges of treason. A year after that he was executed.

Our landlords gave us notice. Mum had trouble finding anyone who would rent her an apartment or give her a job. When she eventually succeeded in both, she didn't earn enough money to look after all of us and Santigi too. So Santigi found work elsewhere, and he came every Sunday to wash our clothes even though Mum couldn't pay him. He told me often that he would keep coming until the day I graduated from university. And he did.

In time, Mum remarried and Santigi was given a job as head steward in the new household. But by then he had begun to drink. He had one failed marriage and then another, each producing a daughter. He named the first Yabome and the second Memuna Aminatta after my sister and I. Santigi showed little interest in either girl. Eventually, Memuna Aminatta's mother met a man who made her happy and she disappeared from our lives. His first wife, Marion, married again too, but remained a friend to Santigi, although it's hard to say whether he deserved her loyalty. What it was Santigi was searching for at the time, I don't know. He dyed his hair with boot polish, and when he sweated in the heat, the polish ran down his face. He insisted he was younger than he was, until he knocked so many years off his age that, if he were to be believed, he would be younger than my stepmother and soon almost as young as my elder brother, on whom he almost certainly had twenty years. He became a figure of fun among the children in the neighbourhood. And he kept on drinking. He remained trustworthy in every way, except one. When my parents were out, he helped himself to the contents of the liquor cabinet. He frequently turned up to work intoxicated and, after several warnings, my stepfather lost patience and Santigi was suspended.

Santigi did everything to win his job back. In Sierra Leone there exists a custom whereby a person of lower status who has offended a person of higher status will appeal to someone of equivalent or, better still, even greater status than the offended party, will plead for that person to intercede on their behalf. To 'beg' for them, is what we say in Krio. In the decades he had lived and worked with my family, Santigi had met dozens of people of influence and he remembered them all. Now he visited their homes, waiting patiently for an audience. He explained the circumstances of his suspension, persuaded each of his contrition and asked them to 'beg' my stepfather on his behalf to have the suspension lifted. My stepfather would tell the story amidst much laughter—how for weeks to come at every cocktail party, lunch or dinner he attended, every restaurant he entered, or so it seemed, somebody came up to him to discuss Santigi's case. My stepfather, however, remained adamant, until one day he attended an international banking conference. As the delegates gathered, the governor of the state bank approached him and asked if they might have a word. My stepfather thought the governor must have something confidential to discuss. They stepped aside. In a low voice the governor said: 'It's about your steward, Santigi.'

Santigi was found a job as a messenger in the offices where my stepfather worked. The job gave him a decent income and a pension, and it removed him from the dangers of the liquor cabinet. Santigi still dyed his hair and now he wore dentures too; he also lied on his application form about his age, partly perhaps out of vanity, but also no doubt believing this might give him an advantage. What it meant was that he was obliged to continue working well after his retirement age.

Santigi would live to see the country all but destroyed by war and survive the invasion of Freetown by rebel forces in 1999. When I returned home in 2000, he was there to greet me. I kissed him and he seemed overcome with shyness. I wrote of him and my cousin Morlai, who was there that day to greet me too, in the memoir of my family which I published two years later, 'I remember them both as confident lads: the flares, the sunglasses, the illicit cigarettes, the slang.' Santigi didn't say much during our reunion. He watched and listened awhile as Morlai and I laughed and chatted and then he picked up the pair of chickens Morlai had brought as a gift to me and slipped away to the back of the house. When I published the book, a launch was held in Freetown, at the British Council. It was a formal occasion, as book launches in Sierra Leone generally are. Santigi turned up drunk. I gave him his own

signed copy. He kissed it and slapped me on the back and
kept on slapping me on the back, hearty blows, even when I
was trying to sign books. I saw Santigi a good few times over
the years to come; he would visit when I was home. Not once
was he sober. Mum didn't want me to give Santigi money. She
said he spent it on moonshine, so I gave the money to Marion
for his daughter Yabome instead.

Santigi's life began to crumble fast. He gave up his little
house in Wilberforce and started moving from one rented
room to another. He had retired by then and Mum could
no longer contact him at the bank. She lost track of where
he lived, but never entirely; if too many months went by, she
always sent for news, and somebody somewhere could always
tell her Santigi's whereabouts. He came to visit less often. It's
strange how some people's stories always end the same way.
Perhaps a clue comes from my cousin Morlai, who also began
to drink at the same time as Santigi—it was after my father's
execution. 'It felt like we were going back into the darkness,'
he told me. My brother told me that years ago when he helped
Santigi clear out his little house in Wilberforce, there among
his possessions were dozens of pictures of my father, from
snapshots to pictures torn from newspapers. A near-death
experience while he was drunk shocked Morlai into sobriety.
He married and had children. He grew back into himself,
stronger this time. Today he's a successful businessman, and
although those things that happened to our family meant
Morlai was never able to finish college, all his own children
have done so. For whatever reason, even though we loved him,
for Santigi redemption never came.

On my last visit home to Freetown I arrived to discover
Santigi had had a stroke two weeks earlier. In the weeks that

followed, Mum and I tried to get him moved to a care home, but he died before that could happen. So we bought him a coffin and all his neighbours chipped in to pay for a suit from the second-hand clothes stalls at Government Wharf. I had never seen Santigi in a suit, and I asked Mum what he looked like. She laughed softly and told me he looked good. I was back in England on the day of his funeral. I couldn't go, so I sat at my desk and I did what writers do. I wrote this instead.

1979

In the land of Ferdowsi, Rumi and Omar Khayyam, Hafez and Scheherazade, in October of the year 1977, fifty-nine poets and writers assembled to read and recite for ten continuous nights. Ten thousand people gathered in the gardens and halls of the Goethe Institute in Tehran. The stories and poems were recorded and distributed to ten times ten thousand people. In the course of those nights, under the bright stars and moon of the city's cloudless skies, the nation's intellectuals joined chorus with peasants, workers and mullahs who raised their own voices in protest in towns and cities across the land. Two hundred and eighteen poems were read, and in the words they chose the poets spoke their anger to the Shah, to where he sat upon his Peacock Throne. The Shah grew vexed, and in the weeks that followed, he tried to crush the people, but the people would not be crushed. And so he tried to appease them, he blamed his prime minister and sent him away, he repealed some laws and made new ones. But still, the people would not be appeased. A year later, the Iranian people had had enough of twenty-five hundred years of monarchy. There were more protests and strikes. By summer of that year, the

Shah had squarely entered the business of making martyrs. On September 7, he put the country under curfew, and when protesters gathered in Jaleh Square, he unleashed his security forces upon them. Hundreds were killed.

My family—mother Maureen, stepfather, elder brother and sister, my younger brother and I—arrived in Tehran a year later, posted there by the United Nations, for which my stepfather worked. I was fourteen, and about to see a part of somebody else's history being made. I wish I had been older, wiser. I wish I could remember more, had paid more attention, understood more—but then I remind myself that I was not alone. What happened in 1979 has happened many times before and many times since, in places where people have set themselves free and believed with all their hearts that the freedom they had fought for was real and lasting, only to be recaptured.

Winter 1978

My sister and I flew Pan Am to Tehran from boarding school on December 15, 1978. Due to snow on the ground in England, our train had been unable to reach the platform, and so we disembarked and plunged into two feet of snow, struggling with our suitcases along the tracks. We would have missed our plane, had it not also been delayed several hours because of the weather.

In Iran, the workers of the National Oil Company had been on strike since the massacre in Jaleh Square. Kerosene and heating oil were in short supply, and our house in Ehteshamiyeh Street was freezing. We had a row of juniper trees at the end of the garden and a view of the Elburz Mountains.

We knew scarcely a soul, had no television. There would have been little point; the programmes were all in Farsi. We listened to the BBC World Service and Voice of America for reports of what was happening in the country: the roadblocks, the soldiers, the graffiti, the curfew, the power cuts.

I was, at the time, an ardent revolutionary. I had a poster of Che Guevara on my wall and a sweatshirt bearing his image. I read his speeches and admitted to no one that I found them utterly impenetrable. I was ardent—all I lacked was a revolution. And now here was a revolution and I had no idea whose side I was on. The Shah was a tyrant who controlled the nation's wealth and tolerated no opposition. From our house we often drove past Evin Prison, where the political detainees were held, and they included intellectuals and artists. Confusingly, the Shah also had a reputation as a social progressive who believed in the education of women, and planted trees.

Khomeini was unappealing and, as a religious leader, disbarred himself from my support. But when I heard people on the radio warning that the Communists would take over from the mullahs if there was a revolution in Iran, I decided to back the rebels. I spent my evenings reading by candlelight before taking a freezing shower (if there was water, which often there was not) with which I tried to imbue myself with revolutionary spirit. I fell asleep huddled under blankets and woke to clear blue skies and the startling sight of the mountains.

Pahlavi Avenue (now Valiasr or Vali-e Asr Street) was the main thoroughfare through the city, and it seemed every other street or building was named Pahlavi something: Pahlavi Square, the Pahlavi Institute. Reza Shah and his son, Mohammad Reza Pahlavi, had built modern Tehran and wished their efforts to be acknowledged. Not long after starting in his new post, my stepfather was invited to present his credentials to Mohammad Reza Pahlavi, whose titles were strung across the top of the crested card: 'His Imperial Majesty, King of Kings, Light of the Aryans, Head of the Warriors.'

In the Tehran of 1978, there was Kentucky Fried Chicken, an Ice Palace rink, Polidor Cinema, the City Theatre and a casino in the Hilton Hotel. We visited none of those places. The city was in virtual lockdown, and many venues were no longer open or open only on certain days. The Shah had tried to placate the mullahs by closing coffee shops and banning the sale of alcohol. We visited the bazaar where my mother bought vegetables from a green-eyed Kurd whose stall faced the street. Trouble often kicked off at the bazaar, stoked by the *bazaaris*, the merchant class who had dominated trade and imports until the Shah allowed himself to be courted by foreign interests. The main bazaar in Tehran became emblematic of the *bazaaris'* loss of influence to the executives of multinationals and was a flashpoint for protests. The inside of the bazaar was a web of shadowed alleyways where getting lost was all too easy, so we dared peek only from the relative safety of the street at the ubiquitous carpets, cassettes, plastic flowers, heaps of rose petals and saffron.

There was nothing to do. Everything that might have made life more bearable—our stereo, our books—was held up in a shipment along with the rest of our household goods. One day the telephone rang, even though there was nobody who was likely to call us. I picked it up, but there was no sound save the distant murmur of male voices. I told my stepfather, who remarked that the line was very likely bugged. SAVAK, the Shah's secret police, were known to be very thorough. In my boredom, I would sometimes pick up the phone and listen: they were always there, the tiny, tinny voices, like a madman's mutters. Often, I'd yell or sing or whistle, but there was no response. It was a household with three cold and bored teenagers, and we bickered and bitched. It snowed, and for a couple of days we were trapped. I built a snowman with my five-year-old brother while men shovelled snow off the roof. In a photograph of us separated by the looming snowman, you can catch a glimpse of my Che Guevara sweatshirt under my woollen jacket.

Winter bore down on us. We kept the windows of our house sealed tight against the cold, which is perhaps why, at first, we didn't hear the singing. Or perhaps, it had just taken a while for the singing to reach our suburb of Darrous, where the avenues were wide and the walls high. Fury with the Shah had spread from the poor of south Tehran to the wealthy in the northern suburbs. People took their rage and fashioned it into a song, and at night they sang it from the rooftops to others who caught the tune and sang it back.

From somewhere far off a single voice, then a moment of silence. From close by a chorus of voices, some young, some old, a family. From elsewhere, other voices answered. Soon the night was filled with sound. The same thing in every city, town and village across the land, the nights before, that night and every night from then on. I came to know when it would happen. I waited and listened. At the approach of nine o'clock, people turned out the lights, dimmed kerosene lamps, blew out candles and climbed the stairs to their roofs, and I would turn out my light too. For precisely ten minutes, they sang a nightly recitative, the sound of people calling to God for their freedom: two words, two notes, five syllables, each stretched until it resonated like a string:

'Allah-hu Akhbar!'

Curfew Parties

There are two kinds of curfew party. At one you arrive just before curfew and leave at dawn. The other kind requires a little more imagination. Guests arrive dressed to the nines in broad daylight, sip martinis at two in the afternoon and depart before curfew. We received an invitation to a New Year's party of the second kind from the mother of a school friend, Mrs P., an expatriate Dane married to an Iranian. She ran a bakery in town which remained open, indeed thrived, as these places are reputed to do in troubled times, trading cinnamon Danishes, chocolate dainties and a few moments of oblivion.

The party gave us something to look forward to. New Year's Eve fell on a Sunday, a working day in Iran. Nowruz, the Iranian New Year, falls at the beginning of spring, so the day of our party was otherwise just an ordinary day. My mother, brothers, sister and I went into town, for what reason I cannot remember, and were on our way home when we ran into a demonstration of thousands on Pahlavi Avenue. Our driver, Alibaba, turned the car around and headed for the British Embassy on Ferdowsi Avenue, where the huge metal gates were just being closed. The guards let us in and then locked the gates, backing a Land Rover up against them. We waited by our car, swapping stories with others also temporarily seeking sanctuary.

At first the drama pleased us, but what should have been exciting soon became boring. By about one o'clock, we began to worry about getting to the party, due to begin at two. In decades to come I would read about people in Sarajevo who risked the fire of snipers to sit in a cafe and drink coffee. I would understand exactly why a person would do such a thing. In the places I grew up—Sierra Leone, and also Nigeria, Zambia and Iran because that's where my stepfather's job took us—curfews and coups were depressingly common; in Sierra Leone, we seemed to live in a perpetual state of emergency. In the final years of the 1991–2002 war there, ordinarily sane friends would risk their lives for a last drink in a favourite bar and drive home without headlights, skirting the army checkpoints. I did it myself.

In Iran, in the winter of 1978, after less than a month of confinement in Tehran, getting to the party became of the utmost importance. My mother asked that the embassy gates be opened. The security staff reluctantly complied. A great deal of reversing, manoeuvring and tutting ensued. When we set off down Ferdowsi Avenue, we just about had time to get home and change, but at the Shahyad Tower (soon to be renamed the Freedom Tower), we ran into the protest again. This time we had no option but to drive on. People banged on the roof of the car and thrust their faces at the windows. Sweat rose on the back of Alibaba's neck as he edged the vehicle forward. Down a side street a car burned. We never should have put Alibaba in that position; all the same, thanks to him, we made it through. At home my stepfather reported troubles of his own, having been besieged in his office while a mob gathered outside and loudly contemplated burning the building down. He'd gone out, located the ringleaders and addressed them in Arabic, though he spoke the language quite badly, having learned it long ago when he first joined the UN, along with Esperanto, which the organization had all its staff learn for a while, with the perfectly logical and democratic but ultimately unpopular idea that it might become the UN's official language.

We were late. From the outside there was no evidence of anything taking place inside the house. I don't even remember seeing cars with their waiting drivers; people must have driven themselves. The road was quiet, though probably that spoke more to the wealth of the area than the unrest elsewhere. Inside, the house had an air of an enchantment. Guests drank champagne, whiskey and good wine. Our hostess wore an oyster-coloured satin gown that left her shoulders bare. The heavy drapes were drawn tight and not a ray of sun broke through. Beneath high ceilings, we gathered round tables laid with crystal and silver. We ate guinea fowl and saffron rice sprinkled with slivered almonds and raisins. There was music; we danced into the night, or so it seemed. Except it wasn't night. Such was the success of the party that we all forgot about the curfew. Around a quarter to eight there was a terrific scramble as guests made for their vehicles. My stepfather was driving. There was no street lighting, and Tehran is anyway virtually impossible for a visitor to navigate. Somehow, getting lost had been written into the poetry of the day, the final stanza. The first thing we did was to argue, but as the minutes passed, we grew nervous and shut up. Everyone pitched in, trying to work out the route. We drove past the same street sign twice; nothing looked familiar. We'd no idea what part of town we were in. Then we ran into a checkpoint and a soldier stepped into the headlights and waved us down. Even if he didn't shoot us, our chances of making it home by curfew were now just about zero. My stepfather spoke to the soldiers in fitful Arabic. Arabic is not even a bit like Farsi, and the Iranians are proud of the difference, but I guess a good many people in Iran went to Koranic school and studied Arabic there. The soldier pointed us in the right direction. We shouted with relief when we recognized Ehteshamiyeh Street. At one minute to eight, we turned into our front gate. The party expedition had united us—never more so than in that single minute.

Then we got inside, turned on the lights and decided it wasn't such a big deal—we would have made it home safely anyway.

Chocolate, Exile and Return

At my boarding school in England, we had a tradition that any overseas girl belonging to a country which had chosen to implode was given permission to stay up late and watch the news reports of it doing so in the housemistress's apartment. Two days after I left Tehran for the new school term, the Shah and his family left too, saying they were going on an extended vacation. Along with the Iranian girls, I was called downstairs in my dressing gown to watch the news. We carried our mugs of cocoa with us, and so my memory of the Shah's defeat comes with the taste of chocolate. The Shah left at night, and there was no news footage of the occasion, but I remember a photograph of him and the Empress Farah, which I suppose must have appeared in the newspapers around that time. The Empress is wearing a fur hat and a coat with a fur collar and holding a pair of gloves. Behind her are half a dozen men in dark suits. The Shah is holding a hat in his left hand. They are a procession, but one which is proceeding nowhere because a man in a military uniform has dropped to his knees in front of the Shah and is trying to kiss his feet. The Shah is bent towards the man, as if to raise him up, as if this act, which has been performed many times by countless others, is now embarrassing for him. What's odd about the photograph is that the Empress appears to be laughing. A long time later I read that when the Shah was leaving, his imperial guard tried to prevent him. I think that's who the man in uniform must be.

A fortnight later I was back drinking chocolate in the housemistress's apartment to watch Ayatollah Khomeini's jet land at Mehrabad Airport. Senior air force commanders loyal to the exiled Shah begged him to permit them to shoot the plane down. As no airline would risk having him on board as a passenger, the Ayatollah had been obliged to charter a craft from Air France. The plane circled Tehran three times before it landed. There were scenes of jubilant expectation. And then, there on the TV screen, standing at the top of the aircraft steps was the Ayatollah: a man seemingly composed entirely of a black turban, a white beard, a long black gown and a pair of astonishing eyebrows. His image, painted on walls all over Tehran and now held high on the placards of the waiting masses, had become as iconic as the one of Che Guevara on my sweatshirt. Standing next to the captain of the aircraft, the Ayatollah was unsmiling. Shortly before take-off, a foreign journalist had asked him how he felt. He replied: 'How I feel? Nothing.'

Summer 1357

I returned to Iran twelve centuries before I left. According to the entry and exit stamps on my passport, my last visit to the country had taken place in 2537. The Imperial calendar had been replaced with the Islamic calendar since then, so the stamp in my passport gave the current year as 1357. It was 1979.

We were invited to lunch at the home of an Iranian couple. At the door rosewater was sprinkled on our heads, and we were offered fennel seeds and mint. Later we ate lamb on the balcony and in the shade of pomegranate trees. A woman called N asked if she might join me. I was at an age when I was still surprised when anyone addressed me directly; moreover, N asked questions and actually listened to my replies, my views of the Revolution. She was pretty, with a few strands of silver in her auburn curls; she laughed and spoke with her hands. She was an artist and a supporter of the Revolution, a left-winger whose father had been imprisoned under the Shah. N had recently returned from California to set up studio in Tehran. One of her paintings hung on the wall of the house. She led me through to the sitting room to see it: a huge piece, heavy streaks of red paint on a dark background. When it was time to go, we gave N a lift, and she sat in the front seat, flirted with my stepfather and told my elder brother he was handsome. We dropped her off and she dipped her head back inside the car and invited my brother to have lunch with her the next day without bothering to include the rest of us. I watched her walk away. I had never met a woman like N.

At midday her car and driver arrived to collect my brother and much later that afternoon I sat on the veranda and waited for him to come back. I wasn't jealous; I wanted to know about his day, but all he would tell me was that they had had lunch.

Of all the people I met in Tehran at that time, N seemed to embody the spirit of 1979. That summer the Revolution still belonged to everyone; after the repression of the Shah's era, the artists, the poets, the writers were heady with the possibilities of liberty.

Gone was January's dark and frigid city. This year Nowruz had brought a truly new beginning. The mood in Iran was euphoric, and the whiff of freedom still hung like the smoke of fireworks in the air. The Shah had taken with him the curfew, the power outages, the water shortages. Mrs P's pastry shop was open, and people queued to buy her dainties as before. The bazaar was open. We had a swimming pool and in the dry heat of the Tehran summer I spent my days diving in and out of the water. A hedge of cypress trees separated our house from the one next door and where there was a gap I would sometimes see a boy—a young man really—watching us swim. On occasion I would nod or wave and he would wave back. One day I said hello and told him my name. I assumed he lived in the house next door but discovered later that he was the caretaker's son. He didn't speak any English and so we went back to nodding and waving.

One day he appeared at the gap in the hedge with a friend around his own age. By then my sister had joined us from a stay in France. She was nearly seventeen and newly sophisticated; the friend spoke English, had a motorbike and a quiff. He gave us each a ride around the block. Another time he turned up in a car (borrowed, as the bike had been) and we went driving around the neighbourhood with no destination in mind. A few streets from home we ran into an impromptu roadblock. The checkpoints were no longer manned by the army but by the Komiteh, or Revolutionary Committees, who operated under the auspices of the mosques and drew their membership from the local youth. During the Revolution, the Komiteh had been Khomeini's foot soldiers: whipping up protests, acting as vigilantes, tracking down supporters of the Shah's regime, issuing beatings. Increasingly, they saw it as their role to enforce the new Islamic orthodoxy and arrested people arbitrarily for anti-revolutionary behaviour. The ones who stopped us were young, wore jeans and T-shirts and carried automatic weapons. They crowded around the car and several of them leaned in through the windows, staring at us. They demanded to know what we were doing.

Our companions began by joshing, if a little nervously. They reached out of the window and shook hands with a few of the Komiteh guys. Cigarettes were offered and accepted but not lit. The boys still didn't let us through. A lot of questions were being asked, that much was evident, though the conversation was entirely in Farsi. Our friends offered wordy explanations, upturned palms, apologetic shrugs and lot of nods and some headshaking. Once they even turned to look at us in the back of the car as if surprised to find us there. Finally, one of the checkpoint guards took a step backward and I saw that they were going to let us go, the rest stood clear of the car, but they didn't raise the barrier. Our driver executed a swift three-point turn and we drove straight back home.

I have long been interested in beginnings: to trace things back to the first flap of the butterfly's wings that culminates in the hurricane. I wonder if my interest originated in Iran when I was fifteen years old and I saw how when things start, they start small. The summer of 1979, the butterfly had already taken to the air. Liberals and left-wingers, secular Muslims and non-Muslims had supported Khomeini because they believed him when he said he had no desire for power and they believed only he could muster the authority to oust the Shah. Be careful what you wish for. But when you are in prison you will wish for anything other than to be in the place you find yourself. Shortly before we were stopped by the Komiteh, the clergy

had tried to force an edict through the provisional government which would oblige women to wear Islamic attire in the
workplace; they'd backed down in the face of protest. By then
beaches and sports events had become segregated; the huge
swathes of grey were all those parts of everyday life in which
behaviour had not yet been mandated by the law: men and
women walking, dining, driving together, men and women
talking to each other. What I had witnessed at the checkpoint
was a show of strength. The Islamists were gradually gaining
power over the liberals in the government and in the streets.

A viscous silence had filled the car, but by the time we
got home the boys were trying to make light of what had
happened. They only tapped their forefingers to their temples
and shook their heads. Thus, we neglected to learn our lesson,
and instead we went for a swim in the pool at my parents'
house, laughing and splashing until the enraged caretaker
burst through the hedge and ordered us all out of the water.
That evening when my stepfather came home I ran down
the steps to greet him, fussing over him under the gaze of
the caretaker, who planned, I believed, to report me to my
stepfather for my behaviour and now waited at the gap in the
hedge for his moment. But I did not leave my stepfather's side
until eventually I saw him give up and turn away.

I was afraid I'd end up having to go with my stepfather
down to the local police station to be reprimanded by the
Komiteh. I think I was also frightened of being thought a
fool. The whole of my adolescence, my transition away from
girlhood seemed marked by a heavy sense that I ought to
know better, should conduct myself with more propriety, be
more dignified. I now seemed capable of earning disapproval
simply by being the way I had always been. I had swum with

boys hundreds of times, including that summer in our pool. I'd never ridden on a motorbike or in a car alone with boys before, and now I had done so with dramatic consequences. I could not work out what I would say in my defence, or indeed exactly what it was I was being charged with.

In the end nothing bad happened to me. The caretaker never made his report; the only difference was that the next day the caretaker's son was gone. I did not see him again.

Persia

In the early months of the 1979 Revolution the alliances that had brought down the Shah held together, but by summer the liberals, the left-wingers and the hardliners were battling for control of the Revolution. The liberals had already lost but didn't know it yet. The leftists were being edged out, and some were accused of being counter-revolutionaries. The provisional government under Prime Minister Mehdi Bazargan was trying to draft a new constitution and everyone—the women's groups, the clergy, students, writers and artists—wanted a say. The Revolutionary Council, who controlled the Komiteh, was becoming increasingly bullish and the prime minister, Bazargan (who kept trying to resign only to have his offers turned down by Khomeini), had agreed to a power share. There were daily executions: men who had been part of the Shah's regime. Photographs of their corpses appeared on the front page of newspapers: naked barrel chests with grey chest hair, half-open eyes, bloodied faces, unbuttoned flies. In the summer of 1979 hope and vengeance ran hand in hand.

The museums were open again, though, and one day I was invited to visit a small, private collection in one of the suburbs of Tehran. The building had been the house of a wealthy trader a century ago. Inside the courtyard the sound of traffic died away, fountains played. Upstairs in a vast, silent room, I stood before a hunting scene: turbaned men on horseback chased deer; in the centre a lion clawed the back of a gazelle; at the edges fish swam in streams. In another scene a woman reclined in the arms of her lover; a man and a woman rested under a tree; a third man invited a woman to sit by him.

Two countries exist in the space where Iran lies on the map: there is Iran and there is Persia. The Shah's father lovingly recreated Persia, replacing the Islamic lunar calendar with the Persian solar one, purging Arabic words from Farsi and banning the veil. He also set about crafting a modern state out of an underdeveloped land ruled by clerics. His Iran, the one he set about creating, was an oil-rich nation of highways and tall buildings. The Iran of the contemporary Western imagination, on the other hand, is home to a population given to outbreaks of religious hysteria and governed by stern mullahs obsessed with female apparel. None of these countries, of course, really exists. But if you were to look for them, Isfahan is where you might find Persia, while the Holy City of Qom is Iran.

We drove out of Tehran one weekend, along hot tar roads south to Isfahan: stretches of moonscape interrupted by flashes of green, a spread of irrigated fields and quiet groves where once or twice we stopped to picnic and where I saw, for the first time, peacocks in the wild and experienced the sudden shock of their unearthly beauty. In Isfahan, twice capital of Persia, we stayed at the Shah Abbas Hotel which was, as far as I recall, entirely empty of guests apart from us. The hotel, the most luxurious in the city, was built on the site of a fourteenth-century caravanserai when the city was part of the Silk Route. Now it was offering pretty good discounts on account of the lack of business, otherwise I am sure we would never have been able to afford it. Though Isfahan had given its share of martyrs to the Revolution, there was far less evidence of the unrest here: no roadblocks, no graffiti or burned buildings. The turquoise domes of the city's mosques, walls covered in mosaics of the same colour, were reflected in ornamental pools of water. We took photographs of ourselves standing at the entrance *iwan* and wandered through the bazaar.

How melodic a word is 'Isfahan.' Is-fa-han. How short and sharp is the word 'Qom.' The Holy City of Qom is where the Ayatollah lived before exile and where he returned as soon as he stepped off the Air France plane. To Qom and into seclusion, from where he insisted that he did not wish to be leader, just a spiritual advisor to the nation. He never uttered the word 'theocracy.' On our way back to Tehran, after our weekend in Isfahan, we stopped in Qom, in the main square, a huge expanse of dust in my memory, a barren football field, with a few stalls around the edges and people going to and coming from the mosque. Neither my mother, sister nor I were allowed into the mosque unless we were veiled. My mother borrowed a chador from a local stall; my sister and I refused to wear them and so were obliged to wait outside. We stood unchaperoned, unveiled, in the middle of Iran's holiest city, beneath the eye of the sun and of the Ayatollah. Soon enough we began to attract attention. There was no way of forgetting you were female in Iran. In Tehran I'd been groped by a middle-aged man as I took a stroll round our neighbourhood. Whenever we visited the bazaar, Alibaba trotted alongside us, trying to shield our bodies from men's stares with his bulk. Sometimes he even spread his arms out like a chicken protecting her chicks. In

Qom, within minutes our decision not to join our parents and brother was looking decidedly problematic. We folded our arms across our chests and sat on a low wall until a stallholder, the same one who had lent my mother a chador, invited us to conceal our immodesty beneath the awning of his stall.

A few weeks after we passed through Qom, the Italian journalist Oriana Fallaci went to the city to interview the Ayatollah. As a condition of the interview she was told that she must be veiled in the Ayatollah's presence. She complied but then questioned him about the position of women within Islam, and the wearing of the veil in particular, until Khomeini snapped: 'If you do not like Islamic dress, you are not obliged to wear it. Because Islamic dress is for good and proper young women,' which is a pretty funny answer, but perhaps was not intended to be. Fallaci wrenched off her chador and the Ayatollah had her thrown out.

Amrika

If anyone asked, we were to say we were British. People asked quite often, as it happened. Since three of us were brown-skinned, at checkpoints they'd ask if we were American. In Tehran in the summer of 1979 America was the Great Satan; on walls around the city were written the words: *Death to America*, or *Marg bar Amrika*. Soon, saying you were British would become a problem too; after all Britain was the Great Satan's concubine.

We may have distanced ourselves from the Americans in public, but we didn't let that stop us taking advantage of their generosity. The American Embassy occupied a huge, walled compound in downtown Tehran. Most embassies had evacuated non-essential staff by then and my mother, like many diplomatic wives, was drafted in to fill the gaps in administrative assistance, working first at the British and then at the New Zealand Embassy. With only the rump of their staff left in Tehran, the Americans opened up their commissary to the rest of us. The commissary provided Americans posted abroad with the comforts of home. Every US embassy has one and there you can even buy the same canned foods and condiments found in supermarkets in Topeka or Tuscaloosa, as well as American newspapers, magazines, videos, white goods and even—in the Tehran commissary—a motorbike. The day the commissary opened its doors we were there: enthusiastic looters, stuffing our trolley with giant jars of Goober Grape, tins of hot dog sausages, sauerkraut and French's mustard.

Another time, one of the American diplomatic staff invited us to a party at the Embassy. It was a swim party which later turned into a barbecue; someone's leaving do, no doubt. My brother and I spoke to a man with a moustache called Rich, who asked a question that struck us as curious: 'Have you ever been into the town?' It took us a while to work out that he was talking about Tehran, the city we were in. I replied yes, we went into town most days, and in fact, we had travelled through town to reach this party. Rich told us he had never seen Tehran; he spent most of his days in the compound which his apartment abutted. He was a consular officer, charged with responsibility for processing visa applications. Thousands of Iranians wanted to leave the country, not just the supporters of the former regime—the wealthiest of whom had by and large already left—but now others. It was nearly the end of the summer and some people must have begun to get a sense of which way the wind was blowing. The queue to submit visa applications at a hatch in the side of the Embassy building curled round the block like the tail of a cat. Whenever Rich left the compound, he was recognized and mobbed. He longed for home.

I spoke to another guest, an Irishman who had arrived in Iran the year before to manage the racing stables and who now found himself alone in charge of two hundred horses, whose owners, including the Shah, had fled in the first months of the Revolution, followed soon afterwards by the grooms and jockeys, many of whom came from Pakistan. He hadn't been paid for months, and the money to feed the horses was running out. He said I could come and help exercise them if I liked and a few days later I galloped past the empty stands of Tehran racetrack and later walked through block after block of stables, patting each abandoned horse on the nose. I fell in love with Blushing Boy, an Arab grey with delicate nostrils, and the Irishman wasn't joking when he said I was welcome to keep him if I could find a way to feed him.

The last trip our family took was into the mountains to hike. In our group was the New Zealand ambassador Chris Beeby and his wife. Beeby was a ginger fellow, with the rangy frame of a natural walker, and set quite a pace. We climbed in the heat of the day and were wracked with thirst: we had not thought to bring much water, just one small bottle between us. After two and a half hours we reached the summit and began our descent to the stony valley where a river and its tributaries flowed. Nomads camped near the water with their horses and tents made of stitched leather squares; the women wore veils of yellow and pink sprinkled with flowers, which you saw less and less often in Tehran, where the black veil was becoming ubiquitous.

In mid-September, I left to go back to school. A month later Jimmy Carter granted permission for the cancer-stricken Shah to enter America for treatment at a hospital in New York City. On November 4, the US Embassy in Tehran was taken over. Rich and the other guests at the party were among the hostages. My parents had been camping in the Turkoman steppes the weekend before with Chris Beeby and several Americans who worked at the Embassy, among them the chargé d'affaires. On the way back, the Land Rover broke down and they were late home, and so the Americans had stayed with them that night, all except the chargé who went on saying she had to open the office the next day. She was taken hostage and remained captive for 444 days. The next day Chris Beeby hid the four American guests under blankets in the back of his Chevrolet and drove them to the New Zealand Embassy. For a few days my mother smuggled food from home to them, sworn to secrecy she told nobody, not even my stepfather. Beeby consulted with the Canadian and British ambassadors, and between them they decided that their best chance was to try to pass the American diplomats off as Canadians. They were moved to the home of the Canadian ambassador and issued Canadian passports and exited the country with the aid of the CIA—the story became the subject of the film *Argo*. When the movie came out my mother was angry with Ben Affleck for ignoring the roles of the New Zealanders and gave an interview to the newspapers. In Tehran she spent her remaining days at the New Zealand Embassy shredding documents and taking an axe to the code machine. My stepfather was allowed into the US Embassy building to check on the welfare of the hostages; I saw him once on the news, filmed as he left the building. Rich, or Richard Queen, as I discovered his name to be, was taken gravely ill and released some months later. He was carried out on a stretcher. I don't think the news report gave his name, but I recognized his moustache.

November 5, the day after the storming of the US Embassy, the moderate prime minister, Bazargan, resigned and fled. The Revolutionary Council took control of the government and the country. On November 6, Khomeini gave his blessing to the student kidnappers. The remaining Western embassies closed their missions, as did the UN. For us, it was over.

The Shah died the next summer. At times I remember Iran the way you do a former lover whose name you hear being spoken by somebody else. A decade after we left, following dinner in a Thai restaurant one rainy evening in London, I recognized the people standing a few yards away who had left the restaurant at the same time: the Empress Farah, her daughters, the crown prince. I watched as they hailed a taxi and disappeared. Again, after I moved to the Washington, DC, area, out for dinner in a Turkish restaurant run by a famous chef, I turned and there was Farah Diba, sitting at a circular table with perhaps six other people. She lives now in Maryland, not so far from me. There are exiles in this area who love her still, because on New Year's Day 2020 I went with friends to a nearby Iranian restaurant. From the outside the place was unremarkable, but it came with good reviews and when we opened the door we found it packed with Iranian families, and on the wall huge portraits of the Shah and Farah Diba in their days of glory.

I have tried for a long time to discover what happened to N. I remember both her first name and surname as clearly as I remember her face; I have searched for her on the Internet, but no search has ever produced an Iranian artist of that name. I hope she got out before it became impossible to do so; the country Iran was to become had no place for a woman like her.

I saw the Irish racehorse trainer once more, when he came to ask my mother to help him out of the country and gave me a vivid account of his escape from the Komiteh who appeared at the stables, he said, to arrest him. They set fire to his office. Before he fled, he ran through the stable blocks and loosed the horses rather than leave them to burn or to starve to death locked in their pens. Sometimes when I think of Iran, the summer of 1979 before a people's hard-won freedom was scattered by the wind, I imagine the Arab horses galloping through the suburbs of the city, past the houses and the factories towards the desert—and pray that they at least never were recaptured.

Technicals

In the final years of the war in Sierra Leone I flew back. Like many returnees I had come to help members of my family caught up in the fighting, which by then had lasted more than a decade. The village where my family lived had been behind enemy lines. To reach them we needed to rent a car, preferably a four-wheel drive, but available vehicles were scarce. Eventually I secured one: a black Toyota 4x4 with tinted windows. We departed Freetown at dawn, drove along and around roads cratered by shellfire. In the late afternoon we had reached the dirt track to the village. What struck me most was the emptiness, the absence of people. Occasionally, in the distance, we saw men repairing damaged roofs, but along roads where I was used to seeing schoolchildren, women toting loads, men on bicycles—we did not pass a soul. Then, rounding a corner: a small group of women carrying firewood. We slowed for them, but instead of waving and greeting us, they dropped their loads and ran into the bush. We laughed. We thought we had merely surprised them. Then the same thing happened again. And then again. Women saw our approaching vehicle and fled in silence. We looked at ourselves through their eyes:

deep-throated engine, darkened windows, alloy wheels. The kind of vehicle a rap artist might drive. The kind of vehicle the rebel militia might drive.

The women had been running for their lives.

When I was a kid, we were driven to school every day in a Land Rover. A decade out of British rule, we maintained a high regard for the possessions of the overlord. The Sierra Leone army inherited British army vehicles: the stripped-down Defender—light, rugged, possessed of almost rigid suspension—made for fighting men and we schoolchildren who bounced on our arses on the bare benches in the back.

Over the years the Land Rover was replaced with new objects of desire: the Nissan Pathfinder, the Patrol, the Toyota 4Runner, the ever popular Hilux, flatbeds and pickups in all their forms, and finally the Peugeot 504. King of the African Road throughout the 1970s, these saloon cars became the continent's most popular bush taxi.

Defender. Patrol. These names invoke violence, force. Protection, the manufacturers would doubtless say. Discovery, 4Runner, Pathfinder: adventure, boldness, machismo. Land Cruiser: the big beast of Third World wars, would become the status symbol of the top brass, of Osama bin Laden, the UN, the world's NGOs.

By contrast, the name of by far the most widely used technical vehicle seems less of a fit. Hilux. Hi-lux. 'Hi' as in 'high riding.' Lux meaning luxury. 'The vehicular equivalent of the AK47,' a former US army ranger told *Time* magazine. A rigid steel frame construction with a cab and body fitted on the top. Beloved of farmers, construction crews, rebel armies, warlords, Somali pirates and Afghan insurgents. Good for moving workers, good for moving contingents of men. Mount a machine gun on a tripod on the back and you have a gunship. The design of the Hilux on the battlefield has proved a perfect and unintended synthesis of form and function. Fast. Manoeuvrable. High ground clearance. Light enough to cross minefields without detonating mines, it's said. So popular, they even named a war after it: the Libya-Chad 1980s 'Toyota War' was fought with cavalries of Hiluxes.

When I was writing about Croatia, a friend, a war correspondent who had reported the conflict in the former Yugoslavia, pointed out something which later seemed so obvious I wondered how I could have missed it. 'The reason that war kicked off so fast,' he said, 'was because they were a nation of hunters. Every man had a gun and knew how to use it.' When people go to war, they fight with whatever comes to hand. In Sierra Leone every man was a farmer, every man owned a cutlass or a machete. In Sierra Leone, before the war, if you saw a gang of men in the back of a Toyota Hilux carrying machetes, you'd think they were farmworkers on their way to clear the bush.

A few years later, you'd be running for your life.

Crossroads

In London, in 2013, I boarded a plane bound for Washington, DC. I passed through business class, where the passengers were mainly white men, the world's officer corps. In economy, as I waited for the people in front of me to stow their baggage and ease into their seats, I looked around. It was a full flight. Dotted among the white faces were a good many black ones; DC is a city with a majority Black population. I looked at the passengers and thought: My God, the ancestors of the white people on this plane enslaved the ancestors of the Black people and brought them to America.

A crime so large and yet there they were, the perpetrators and victims, reading in-flight magazines and sipping water from plastic cups. I don't know what prompted the thought, or why it did not strike me every time I travelled to the United States. I would like to say I ruminated for a while, but I didn't. In the next few minutes I found my seat and like everyone else I embarked upon the routine of figuring out how best to organise my blanket, pillow, laptop, book and headset.

Two years later I moved to the DC area to live. This is not the first time I have lived in the United States. I spent a year in the 1990s in the Bay Area and more recently two semesters teaching in Western Massachusetts. It's not my first time in DC either; I've come here at least five or six times on book tours and visits. This, though, is my first time living here.

The summer of 2015 arrived by another name. It was the summer that echoed with the names of Trayvon Martin, the summer of Eric Garner, of Freddie Gray, of Sandra Bland. It was the first time many of us heard of the movement Black Lives Matter. In Britain, in the months before our departure, we watched as in city after city across the United States, Black people rose in protest against the police. Fury ignited neighbourhoods. By the time we arrived in late July, my enthusiasm for the move to America had tempered. In my family we wear differently coloured skins. I am brown, my husband is white, our then five-year-old son is brown. As I say, I had lived in America before, but perhaps it was the news events of the summer that made me feel differently this time, or the fact of having a child, someone to whom one must try to explain the workings of a world which frequently make no sense. I dread, as all parents of Black children do, the day my son understands that the deal life handed him is not the same as the deal life has handed other of his friends. That hurting him is, for some people, a form of sport.

My apprehension was heightened by the surprisingly forceful opinions some American friends offered about where we should live. 'You want to live in the District,' 'Live in Maryland,' 'Whatever you do, don't live in Virginia' (Virginia being the South). A white woman instructed me not to live in Georgetown. Georgetown is the area that grew up around the old port and, with its tree-lined roads and prettily painted row houses, is delightful. Why on earth would anyone not want a home there? 'You don't want to live next door to ageing white people, do you?' I said, many members of my family and my husband's family were, in fact, ageing white people. What I was really thinking was: I'll live where I damn well please.

DC is one of the most segregated cities in America, split neatly down the middle, Blacks to the east and whites to the west. Some areas are up to ninety-eight per cent Black. Notably, nobody white suggested we live in a black area, just liberal white areas, because without it ever being said, 'Black' means crime and 'Black' means poverty.

As it turned out, Georgetown was unaffordable anyway, as was most of the District. Maryland meant a long commute and with Arlington just over the Key Bridge from George-town, I could walk to work. We went to live in Virginia.

One of the first things I realise about Virginia in the heat of summer is how much it reminds me of Sierra Leone. The Potomac, bounded by vegetation that rises from the shallows, looks like the wide, mangrove-frayed banks of the rivers back home. Nightfall brings with it the whirr of crickets, the call of night birds, the whine of the mosquito. Only the nightly recital of the Freetown dogs is missing. The sounds, which are the sounds of my childhood, are as comforting as they are familiar.

The racially mixed family soon notices upon arriving in DC (well, America really) from London how comparatively rare such diversity has suddenly become. In the first week, a man photographs us as we walk three abreast down the Mall. The last time this happened to me was in London in the 1970s. I was skipping hand in hand with a white school friend. A man holding a camera with a telephoto lens leapt from nowhere and took our picture. We concocted wild stories: that the man was a spy, that he had been hired by prospective kidnappers. The man who takes our photograph on the Mall does so in much the same way as the man forty-odd years before did—he doesn't ask, he walks directly towards us without varying his pace and only at the last minute he raises his camera, like a gun.

The other thing that happens a few times is this: we are waiting together at the head of a queue to fill in or submit some piece of paperwork that our new lives require. The person behind the desk, a white woman in each instance, looks up and says: 'Which one of you is first?' She doesn't simply wave both of us forward, which is what happens most everywhere I have ever been. She says: 'Which one of you is first?' She presumes we are not together, you see. It takes a while for us to figure this out. A couple of times when the queue is particularly long, I take our son outside to play until my husband is called forward and then we join him at the desk. But when I do so I am challenged: 'Can I help you?' and 'Excuse me, ma'am, but I am serving this gentleman.' On this last occasion I am standing next to my husband, so close our shoulders touch, leaning with my elbows on the desk and reading our paperwork upside down. In the mind of the woman behind the desk I am apparently a stranger with no sense of personal space, butting in on the business of an Englishman altogether too polite to drive me away, because that's what absolute strangers do all the time, right? In her worldview it is more likely than that we might be together.

A friend describes how something similar happened to her when she unpacked her weekly shopping at the till in a supermarket, and the teller shouted at her: 'You may not touch that man's food, ma'am!' The man was her (white) husband. Really, you have to laugh. Shortly after arriving in Arlington,

I went for the series of medical tests to which new clients must submit on behalf of their medical insurer. Waiting for a bone density test, I was given a form upon which to declare my ethnicity. Black/White/Hispanic/Other. In Britain, one is typically offered a buffet of choices under 'Mixed.' On the medical form I marked both Black and White because ethnicity has a bearing on bone density and medical science does not observe the 'one-drop rule.' There followed an awkward conversation with the administrator whose computer kept defaulting to 'White.'

Each country has its paradigm of race and America's size and cultural might mean the American paradigm has been widely exported, plus the specific heinousness of the crime against Black people in America lends it an extra authority. It can be hard to explain to people in America that there exist other and different experiences of being black. My cultural interpreters back when I first lived here twenty years ago tended to be people of colour from other lands who had lived longer in America than I had: West Indians, Black Britons, Africans.

You are darker than me, therefore I will call you black. You are paler than me, therefore I will call you white.

In those days, what I found curious was the way some people who were very fair-skinned were nevertheless called 'black' by white people. They called themselves black too, or 'Black,' which to me was a matter of a different order, one rooted in knowledge, family and allegiance. The fact was that, to me, it seemed impossible simply by looking at many light-skinned people of colour to tell if they had any African blood at all. I said so to my African friends, who quietly agreed. A British Jamaican friend warned me that I should not say so in the company of African Americans. The idea of 'passing' made no sense either. If you were light enough to look white, why didn't that make you white? Did I know about the 'one-drop rule' back then? I think so, but the enduring nature of its legacy threw me. Did people really hold on to this way of thinking? Perhaps I should have been more thoughtful, because I did know that enslaved women were raped by their masters. So these then were their light-skinned descendants whose skin served as reminder of the plundering of their great-great-great-grandmothers' bodies.

Behind the denials lies shame on both sides; this is the only answer I have. The result is silence. To me and my husband and child, the young white women, whether or not they knew it, were taking part in a nationwide pretence, saying, We're sorry but you are most unusual, this sort of thing really doesn't happen here (Virginia's anti-miscegenation laws were overturned only in 1967). The light-skinned black people were saying, We do not wish to be reminded of what has happened to us in the past. Only on a recent trip to South Africa have I seen anything similar to the simultaneous separation and evident co-mingling of the races one sees in the United States, the energy expended on the self-deceiving lie that is the narrative of what is 'normal.'

In South Africa I would be considered 'Coloured,' a designation and an entire community created by government decree to sweep into one place the untidy evidence of racial mixing, South Africa's version of the 'one-drop rule.' In West Africa, in fact in pretty much every other African country where I have ever travelled, those fair-skinned African Americans and I would be called 'white.' Filming a documentary in Mali where the brown-skinned Tuareg population is referred to as white,

I tried to explain this to one of my English colleagues, who only continued to insist that this could not possibly be so. It was left to our Bambara fixer to tell him: 'You are in Africa now.' In his view Obama was a white man, though he had travelled and knew this not to be the case in majority-white countries. He stopped a passing waiter, 'Obama,' he asked, 'black or white?' And the waiter replied: 'White.'

Another thing that I have noticed in the US is the battle fatigue I saw first in Black people when I was there in the 1990s, which we in Europe did not (yet) feel. Sometimes this showed itself as a kind of footslogging determination, or angry frustration, other times a withdrawal from the fray. I remember very well a couple I met in San Francisco.

I had gone to interview the wife, about what I can't rightly remember; I was a journalist at the time. I do remember that I had been put in touch by a mutual acquaintance and that the house at which I arrived had an elegant interior and a garden with a flower-bordered lawn. During the interview we, the wife and I, found so much commonality that her husband arrived home to find us in the garden with a bottle of wine. The husband was as handsome and warm as his wife was beautiful, funny and gracious. Within a short time, he was insisting that I should bring my husband for dinner. A little later the conversation turned to race. 'I have nothing against them,' said the handsome husband smoothly. 'But I wouldn't have a white in my house. I work with them and I have no problems with it. But that's where it stops.' I looked over at his wife, who I imagined would surely murmur some sort of admonishment, but she only smiled and offered me more wine. You're wondering if I protested? No. Do I feel guilty about that? Not really. I had never heard anyone talk that way, any person of colour I mean; I've heard plenty of whites say such things. Only there was no bitterness in the husband's voice, just a certain matter-of-factness. I sort of understood. The vigilance required of being Black is too often exhausting; in relationships with white people, the heavy lifting is inevitably borne by the Black person: to circumnavigate conflict, to avoid all evidence of appearing chippy, to keep the white at their ease. The couple from San Francisco had found their own solution. I did not challenge them; I was learning about race in America.

You can imagine, though, that we never did take them up on that dinner invitation.

In Sierra Leone, before the war of 1991–2002, a certain kind of traveller disembarked regularly from flights from the United States, alongside the missionaries and Peace Corps volunteers. Around their necks they wore leather pendants in the shape of Africa, they dressed in shirts and skirts made of printed kente cloth and they had African names, which were not the names they had been given when they were born. They were African Americans come home.

My last visit to Sierra Leone before the war made it impossible was in 1991. In the company of a group of friends I celebrated my birthday at a restaurant called Old Wine, New Skins which had been set up by a family of African American 'returnees' (as we called them then; we would later retrieve the term to describe Sierra Leonians who came home from overseas at the end of the war). They were a man and his three wives—this made some among us roll our eyes, just as we were working to rid ourselves of polygamy. It was even said that one of the wives was white. They opened a restaurant and specialised in cooking our own food and then selling it to expats, which they did rather well, balancing the flavours to satisfy the requirements of authenticity while serving Western tastes. Why hadn't one of us thought of it? The man wore dreadlocks and a *gara* shirt; when he came to take our order, he called us 'sister' and 'brother.' The women wore long robes of Dutch wax print. All night we tried for a glimpse of the 'white wife,' but we achieved none.

If I am truthful, I felt embarrassed for the returnees; to have come all the way here, to our little country dragging itself along the developmental floor, seemed like an act of desperation. I would later feel a similar discomfort in the United States faced with the same longing in African Americans, which found expression in Kwanzaa, books and posters about African kings and queens, tie-dye clothing. They seemed to know more about the history of my continent than I did. They yearned for what I possessed and took for granted, worse still, failed to cherish or perhaps could not cherish. Sierra Leone is a beautiful country: a coastline composed of curved beaches, pale and bright as cutlass blades, iridescent sunbirds that drink nectar from hibiscus cups, city streets lined with trees so heavily jewelled with fruit that in mango season you buy from the street sellers merely to save yourself the effort of reaching up with your own hand. But Sierra Leone is no Eden. People were always trying to fleece the returnees and treated them with contempt. I knew because on the streets sometimes I was mistaken for one of them. There were other reasons, though, why I could not share in the romance. My relationship with my paternal country was an abusive one; I was the daughter of a murdered political activist.

I don't know what happened to the family from Old Wine, New Skins; I'm guessing they left when the fighting came to Freetown in 1997, if they hadn't already gone by then. By all accounts America's evacuation of its citizens was nothing short of masterly. A warship, hulking, appeared and anchored off Lumley Beach; helicopters took off and landed in defiance of the rebel-proclaimed 'no-fly zone' and marines went house to house collecting US citizens. A family friend opened the door to an armed unit come to remove his young son who happened to have dual citizenship. Only if you take me too, he said, and so they whisked him into a vehicle and a short time later he was out of the country. The whole evacuation lasted a mere matter of hours. The family at Old Wine, New Skins must have been grateful then for the eagle on the front of their passports. I wonder where they are now and whether they feel as ashamed for us, for our failure to spare ourselves the descent into hell, angry that we took their dream of Eden and desecrated it so thoroughly that it must have been impossible ever to dream the dream again.

Why did they choose us when others of their countrymen had headed for Ghana, so much more developed, so much more distinguished? These were the days before you could acquire a DNA test for a handful of dollars, but the fact is whether or not they knew it, the family were more likely to share DNA with us than any other peoples on the west coast of Africa. Sierra Leone's other name, the one it was known by to the outside world and for several hundred years, was the Slave Coast. Only a minority of all the slaves taken from West Africa went to North America, most ended up in South America or the West Indies, but of those who went north, a good many came from Sierra Leone and a significant proportion from a single trading fort on a small island just off the coast near Freetown called Bunce Island.

The ruins of a fort stand on Bunce still, surrounded by the rusted corpses of cannons. Great stone walls once enclosed the chief agent's residence, a Georgian-style mansion it is said, complete with a wrap-around verandah in the style of the great plantation houses of South Carolina, formal terraced gardens and even an Orange Walk. An arched doorway led through to rooms with high ceilings, and at the back of the building a false fireplace (false because the temperature in Sierra Leone averages about thirty-five degrees centigrade year-round). The slave yards where the captives were held were just behind the house; the chief agent could keep check on his goods from the upper windows of his home. In 1791, a British woman named Anna Maria Falconbridge dined at Bunce (or Bance as it was then called) Island Mansion and described the sight of the enslaved men and women: 'between two and three hundred wretched victims, chained and parcelled out in circles, just satisfying the cravings of nature from a trough of rice placed at the centre of each circle.' By the time of Anna Maria's visit, the fort was operated by the company of John and Alexander Anderson, having been sold six years before by Grant, Oswald & Company. (Remember the name Oswald, because it will come up again, along with that of Richard Oswald's American trading partner Henry Laurens.) Before that the fort was operated by the Royal African Company, which traded slaves on behalf of the British Crown.

Beneath the fortified mansion there is a cave, once an underground powder magazine, though local folklore says slaves were held there too. Step inside and you feel movement in the warm and stinking air, hear a sound like breathing and the rustle of a thousand wings—the cave roof is thick with bats. Beyond the old magazine a path skirts a series of dunes which, when I first realised that they were in fact eight-foot-high mounds of empty oyster shells, I imagined them to have been tossed from the ramparts by gluttonous Englishmen. Later I learned they were used in the making of lime for the castle walls. If memory serves, the path continues round the perimeter of the tiny island, past a small cluster of graves which mark the last resting place of the white traders who died on Bunce.

Wade into the sea by the small landing beach and before the water has reached your knees you can find rum bottles, wood nails, pottery shards. Within minutes your hands are full of the jetsam and flotsam of slave ships and you throw the lot back into the waves. Standing on the remainder of a small stone jetty, you call to the boatman on the shore who brought you to the island and now waits to bring you back. You watch him manoeuvre his dugout through the waves with a single paddle. You step off the island from the same place and in the same way as did thousands of departing Africans, only you will step off the boat again in a minute or two onto the shore, while they were transferred to the slave ships that lay anchored in deep water, and if they ever set foot on land again, did so thousands of miles away.

There are stories told in Sierra Leone, from centuries before I was born, of men who arrived on our shores, men who built their houses on the sea. These were not ordinary men, but the spirits of drowned corpses. Left long enough in water a black person's skin bleaches white. They had pale hair and green eyes because they ate fish and drank seawater. They captured men and women and carried them across the sea to feed to their god, a great devil who fed on human flesh. At the thought of what awaited them, some of the captives became catatonic. In the literature of the slaving ships it has a name: 'the lethargy.' In the days when the profits of Bunce went to the British Crown, the men and women and children were branded across their chests. R.A.C.E. (Royal African Company of England). RACE. The captives thought they were branded in order to be butchered and eaten like cattle. Catatonia causes the brain to shut down, rendering the sufferer mute and immobile. One theory suggests that catatonia may have once been an evolutionary fear response, originating in ancestral encounters with carnivores whose predatory instincts were triggered by movement. Captives struck by the lethargy often died of starvation, so the slavers stopped branding their prisoners and attached coloured strings to their wrists instead; they hired translators to explain to them what I suppose must have seemed a lesser fate.

For a long time afterwards, people in Sierra Leone thought white people were cannibals. My stepmother remembers stories of cannibals; they were always waiting to catch children who misbehaved. One day she tells me about a colonial officer in her town who used to wait in his official car outside the railway station; she would see him when she and her friends came back from school and sometimes he would wind down the window, call one of them over and try to persuade the girl to enter the vehicle. My stepmother's grandmother warned her the man was a cannibal, and she told her to run away if he ever tried to talk to her. My stepmother watches my expression carefully as she tells me this story.

You ran from cannibals, you avoided the crossroads, the meeting place of the spirits where men and women might be

snatched and carried to the underworld. At night a grandmother urged her granddaughter returning home to the next
village to stay away from the path. Only strangers who did
not know the countryside travelled the paths, slave-raiding
strangers perhaps, and where the roads met was the place the
unlucky traveller was most likely to encounter them.

The slavers were both black and white men, we know this.
But it is the white men, men who could strike fear into the
heart of a person such that she was turned into a creature of
stone, who haunt the imagination.

My grandfather Pa Roke Forna kept five indentured men. My
aunts and uncles tell me this, those of them who were alive
when we had the conversation some years ago. They speak the
names of the men for maybe the first time in decades. It takes
a few moments to reel their minds back all those years, to the
forties and fifties. Foday, several of them remember, seems to
have been a favourite.

We always called my grandfather Pa Roke, but this was not
his name, it was his title. My grandfather was an advisor to
the paramount chief, like a chancellor I suppose. He presided
over matters of law and heard many cases in the court in
Magburaka. When a man who could not pay his debts came
before the courts, Pa Roke sometimes offered to square the
debt out of his own pocket. Now indentured to my grandfather, the debtor would work on his farm until the debt was
paid, which might take months or might take years. This was
how Pa Roke acquired Foday and the other four men. They
worked his lands which surrounded the village of Rogbonko,
where Pa Roke lived with his wives and children.

When I was a child, my father would take us to visit Pa Roke often. I remember being ushered in to say hello and sent to sit outside again; sometimes during those long visits we ate together, gathered around a single dish of rice from which Pa Roke helped himself deftly using only the tips of his fingers while I used a spoon. Apart from saying hello and goodbye, though, we never spoke, for the reason that we did not share a common language. Pa Roke spoke Temne and I spoke only English. It was typical of my parents' generation, who came of age at the same time as their countries and who kept their gaze fixed firmly on the horizon, to neglect to teach their children the languages they grew up speaking. (Also, our circumstances meant I had spent vital years overseas, and had missed the opportunity to acquire the language naturally.) Pa Roke belonged to a world that was disappearing, and I belonged in a future which was yet to arrive. Many years later I would try to remedy the omission and ask my stepmother to teach me Temne; we constructed the grammar slowly together and on long walks because the language lacked a complete orthography. Linguists at Fourah Bay College had been in the process of compiling one when the war struck.

My aunts count Pa Roke's wives aloud and on their fingers. They start with the names of their own mothers and then of the mothers of their brothers and sisters who have died. Whenever there is an impasse, they look to Adama, who seems to have the best memory and is also the eldest. In all, Pa Roke married sixteen women. The first wife was a praying wife, meaning she was the widow of an older brother or perhaps a cousin and had been given the choice, upon her

husband's death, of taking one of his younger male relatives
as a husband or returning to her own family. She had chosen
Pa Roke. The second match was by all accounts a love marriage, and there appears to have been some friction between
this new wife and the first wife (who seemed not to have
stuck to her devotions), because the praying wife soon packed
her bags and left. Among the other marriages, several were
dynastic. Pa Roke was not married to all his wives at once;
he was well into his nineties when he died and had outlived
all but the last. A good few would have died in childbirth,
as did my grandmother Ndora who was chosen personally
by Pa Roke's second wife (she of the palace coup). Nobody
remembers much about her except that she came from the
next village. She was only a sixth wife and she died bearing
her third child.

It is said Pa Roke and Foday shared an enthusiasm for
animal husbandry. Foday was in charge of the animals, though
the farm mainly produced coffee and rice. Over the years and
through the birth and breeding of many sheep and goats, the
two men grew quite close.

In the evenings Foday sometimes kept company with Pa
Roke on the verandah of the big house overlooking the village
square. The third person who joined them on occasion was Pa
Yamba Mela, the diviner whom Pa Roke kept and housed in
the village, even though Pa Roke was, by all other accounts,
a strict Muslim.

Whether the indentured men ever worked their way out
of debt nobody can tell me. For the most part they stayed
on in Rogbonko village. My uncles and aunts are keen for
me to know that the men were well-treated. They recall

Foday's wedding; Pa Roke had paid the bride-gift and covered the cost of all the celebrations. I do not ask whether he added the bill to Foday's debt, nor do I mention what seems evident to me—that Pa Roke now had two workers for the price of one.

What I also learn is that Pa Roke, who would later rule as regent chief on the death of the paramount chief, was once an indentured man himself. In his youth he had been sold into bondage by two of his uncles in order to raise campaign funds for a chieftaincy election in another chiefdom, one in which Pa Roke's mother was a member of the ruling family. In exchange for an unnamed sum, Pa Roke spent two years working some other man's land, just as Foday worked his. That was the way it was—a man could be born noble and owned by another and own men himself, all in the same lifetime and all in the same skin.

In 1997 I take my stepmother, who is then living with me in London after Freetown was overrun by rebel soldiers, to see the movie *Amistad*. We go to a cinema in Notting Hill Gate, a lovely old movie theatre with balconies and red velvet seats, one of the last cinemas where you could still smoke. The film is based on the true story of an uprising aboard the Portuguese slave ship *Amistad*. The rebels were Africans who had been abducted and enslaved from Sierra Leone in 1839. They killed the cook and the captain (in the film they kill loads more people) and ordered the crew to sail them back to Sierra Leone, but before they could make it the ship was sighted and seized by a US navy vessel, the Portuguese slavers were freed and the Sierra Leonians were imprisoned in New Haven, Connecticut.

In the making of the film, the director Steven Spielberg took a decision not to subtitle a good deal of the dialogue spoken by the African actors. Apparently, the purpose of this was to place the audience in the same position as the New Englanders faced with Africans babbling in incomprehensible tongues. The extras—Mendes and Temnes—were recruited from Sierra Leone and clearly rise to the occasion. Also, I suspect there must have been a good deal of repartee, perhaps even some ad-libbing, because my stepmother, who speaks Temne and understands Mende, keeps giggling. The actors had divided the prison cell into Temneland and Mendeland, which the film shows, though without explanation. According to my stepmother, there was a spontaneous and lively trade of insults between the two.

The *Amistad*, with its (by then) illegal cargo, was bound for Cuba, as were many ships from Bunce. Once, on holiday in Havana, I went to an art exhibition where I stood before a print of an African mask. The mask was one of those designed to be worn over the entire head with rings carved into the base; the features of the face were small and keen. It looked just like one I have at home, which has its origins in the women's secret society: the priestess wears it to lead the initiates in dance. I said: 'It's the Bundu devil.' A man standing nearby, a Cuban and the manager of the collective of artists, heard me and told me that it was more than likely exactly what I imagined it to be. I bought the print and carried it home to London.

The slave ships which crossed the Atlantic from Bunce, and which were not headed for Cuba or the West Indies, docked in South Carolina; from there the captives were bought and sold to plantations around the American South. Henry

Laurens* owned and operated Austin and Laurens, the largest slave auction house in the whole of North America; he was Henry Oswald's main trading partner and bought the bulk of Oswald's Bunce Island captives.

Once, in Louisiana, in search of a more detailed understanding of the lives of slaves, I visited a plantation near Baton Rouge. The experience was bizarre. We wandered around the house (rather poky by the standards of a British manor) and peered into glass-fronted cabinets containing not the belongings of the family but examples of the sort of items they would have owned, which were mainly European antiques. Nowhere, inside or out, was there any mention of the slaves who had worked the plantation. We were ushered out by a Black woman in an antebellum crinoline dress. I asked her whether there were any displays about slavery we could see, slave quarters or suchlike. She said: This way. We'd seen a few French collectibles and now we were being hustled out. Finally, in the gift shop I found one slim volume detailing the lives of slaves entitled *We Lived in a Little Cabin in the Yard*, a collection

---

* In 1777, during the American Revolutionary War, Henry Laurens, by then America's envoy to Holland, was captured on the high seas by the British navy and imprisoned in the Tower of London, the highest ranking American official ever so to be. His old friend Richard Oswald interceded on his behalf and even posted bail. After the American victory, the British government appointed Richard Oswald to negotiate the Treaty of Paris. On the other side of the table, along with Benjamin Franklin and John Adams, was Henry Laurens. Together, the old slaving partners struck a deal to return the slaves recruited into the British army back to their owners, a deal scuppered only by the British North American commander Sir Guy Carleton, who refused to hand over the slaves and sent them instead to Nova Scotia, from where the Black Loyalists (as they were called) petitioned to be sent to Sierra Leone. In 1792 fifteen ships carrying 1,196 people sailed from Halifax to Sierra Leone. The Nova Scotians and other Black former slaves from the US and also from Britain would settle there over the coming decades. The houses of the American settlers are there still, in the villages of Bathurst and Regent, slatted wooden houses, often brightly painted. Little pieces of Louisiana carried home.

of oral accounts of surviving slaves undertaken by the Federal Writers' Project.

In New Orleans I discovered the slaves of Louisiana had left behind more vivid evidence of their presence in other places, in the taste of jambalaya. In making jambalaya the rice is simmered with tomatoes, onion and water, the recipe calls for a mix of seafood, chicken and meat. In Sierra Leone we have an almost identical dish we call Jollof rice. You find people enjoying Jollof rice all over West Africa. Jollof, Djolof derived from Wolof, a people of Senegal. Jollof rice is almost certainly the progenitor of jambalaya. At home in Sierra Leone, we often serve Jollof rice with a condiment made of softly fried onions and Scotch bonnet peppers. The New Orleans recipe calls for andouille sausage, which is the French influence. Every cook has his or her own way of making jambalaya; it's more of a concept really, once you have grasped that fact you can make it anywhere with whatever is at hand. In this way jambalaya is like gumbo, the other famous Louisiana dish, which shares the same trademark of mixed meats and fish and the recipe for which was almost certainly carried in the hearts of the enslaved.

In Louisiana some like to make their gumbo with a roux base—the French again—but I won't have any truck with that. The West African way is to use okra. In fact, West African 'gumbo' is really composed mainly of stewed okra into which some pieces of chicken, smoked fish and meat are thrown. First each okra finger must be chopped into small pieces and then the whole thing simmered at length, the dish takes about four hours to prepare from start to finish. It's my homecoming dish. When my stepmother instructs the cooks, she will tell them: 'Use a wooden spoon.' A wooden spoon rather than a metal spoon because wood makes the okra 'draw,' the way I like it best, but for a good many people the glutinous texture of okra is something of an acquired taste. Hence the roux sauce.

The Gullah people who are direct descendants of Sierra Leonian slaves make their gumbo with okra. By the time people from Sierra Leone were settled on Gullah Island, the Slave Coast had been renamed the Rice Coast and slaves from Sierra Leone in particular were prized for their rice-growing expertise. Henry Laurens himself owned several rice plantations. Captives were shipped from Bunce to Savannah to meet the demand, the rice trade grew, and South Carolina became one of the wealthiest colonies in the Americas. But malaria and other diseases, as well as rice, flourished in the tropical climate of the Low Country and sea islands, driving away the white plantation owners who left the running of their estates to a small number of overseers and slaves acting as drivers. Free, relatively speaking, from the influence of white, Christian culture, the slaves held on to their cuisine, their stories and songs.

Joseph Opala, an American anthropologist who did much to stitch together the history of Bunce Island, identified as Mende the language of an old recording of a song sung by an inhabitant of Gullah. The Sierra Leonians of Bunce brought their spirits with them too; the spirits swam, flew and walked on water in pursuit of the scurrying ships to live on in the religions of the Americas, in Candomblé, Santeria, Voodoo. Mami Wata, who offers great wealth to those who glimpse her in exchange for their unborn children; One-Foot Jombie, the bogeyman who frightens children who won't go to sleep; and

Baron Samedi, who holds the power of life and death and is
keeper of the crossroads.

I am kneeling on a compound floor of cracked, red earth, the
sun at its zenith. It must be well over forty degrees centigrade.
It is the year 2000, close to the end of the civil war. Freetown
is crowded with refugees—my aunt Adama is one. The last of
the fighting is taking place near where my family live in the
north, which is also where the Revolutionary United Front
(RUF) have their headquarters. Today she is telling the story of
the echoes of another war. The story, which I will later put on
paper, will take several hours to hear, during which time we,
her listeners, will stand and shake limbs numb from squatting
or sitting, will swipe at the flies that come to drink the sweat
from our skin. Once I will ask my cousin, who is translating
Adama's words for she tells her story in Temne, whether he
wants to take a break and come back another day. No, he will
shake his head, I have never heard this story. The story begins
with these exact words: 'Your great-grandfather Pa Morlai was
a warrior at the time of the Gbanka wars.' Adama tells us the
tale of my great-grandparents Pa Morlai and Ya Beyas and it
goes like this:

Sometime in the 1880s, the chiefs of Temneland were
foolish enough to double-cross a young warrior by the name
of Gbanka whom they had hired to fight the Mende and
force open the trade routes to the Bumpe and Ribi rivers and
thereby gain access to the sea and the British and foreign vessels that bought gold and ivory along the West African coast.
Gbanka was both Temne and Mende and when he lost faith
in his father's Temne people he turned to those of his mother
and fought for the Mende instead. The ensuing wars lasted

many years, particularly once the northern Loko decided to ally with the Mende.

Pa Morlai was a Loko commander whose fighters overran the town of Mamunta deep in Temneland in an area ruled by the Obai Masamunta Akaik (King Great Beard). Mamunta was where Pa Morlai made his base until the wars were ended (by the British who, tired of the disruption to trade, captured and imprisoned Gbanka). With the end of hostilities Pa Morlai headed back north beyond the Katabai Hills to his village of Matoko, accompanied by the retinue of slaves given to him by Masamunta Akaik as part of the peace settlement between the two men.

Among the slaves was one of Masamunta's own daughters, Beyas. Pa Morlai gifted her to his mother for her household and later, at his mother's behest, took Beyas as one of his wives, and together and over time they had three sons and a daughter.

One day a basket-seller arrived in the town square of Matoko. Ya Beyas, as she was now known, recognised the weave and pattern of his *shuku*; they came from her hometown of Mamunta whose weavers are, even now, renowned for their basketry. Ya Beyas asked the *shuku*-seller to carry a message to her family telling them where she was and begging that they free her. This the basket-seller promised to do, but when he returned the next year he had failed to pass on the message, for what reason we do not know. Ya Beyas gave her message to him a second time and waited another year and this time the basket-seller succeeded in his mission.

There were, in those days, strict rules by which a person could be redeemed from slavery. If the terms were met, then that person was free regardless of the wishes of the owner. When two of Ya Beyas' brothers arrived in Matoko, they

presented before a gathering of the chief and elders of Matoko
and Pa Morlai this inventory of items:

Cow, 1
Barrel of palm oil, 1
Sack of rice, 1
Sack of salt, 1
Tie of tobacco leaves, 1
Country cloth, 1
Silver shillings, 4

Once the ceremony had been conducted, Ya Beyas was a free
woman, except that she wasn't, she was still Pa Morlai's wife.
When Ya Beyas said she wanted to go home to Mamunta, Pa
Morlai withheld permission. She had a wound on her foot,
and he insisted she must stay in Matoko under the care of his
healer. When her foot was better Ya Beyas once again told Pa
Morlai she planned to travel to her hometown and to take
their daughter Hawa to accompany her on the journey, but Pa
Morlai refused permission a second time. Hawa was betrothed
to a young man in Matoko, he pointed out, Ya Beyas needed
to stay for the marriage. In the end, though, he did relent and
gave Ya Beyas leave to go home; he appointed their second son
Saidu to be her travelling companion and settled down to wait
for her return. But Ya Beyas never came back.

Pa Morlai set out to follow his wife. The first time he
entered Mamunta he had done so as a warrior at the head of
an army. Now he entered as a suitor, preceded by a young girl
bearing a heavy calabash upon her head. Pa Morlai went to
Beyas' house and broke cola with her brothers, one of whom,
the former heir to Masamunta Akaik, was now king, and he

presented his calabash, the contents of which would certainly have looked very much like this:

Cola nuts (symbol of friendship)
Bitter cola nuts (symbolic of hard times)
Alligator pepper, 1 (seeds to be kept in dried pod for union to hold)
Prayer mat, 1
Tie of tobacco, 1
Needle and thread
Gold
Silver
Precious stones

Pa Morlai had come to give Ya Beyas' family her bride-gift, outstanding now for some twenty years or more. Ya Beyas took the calabash and in so doing accepted Pa Morlai for her husband, this time as a free woman. Some days after the celebrations were over, Pa Morlai decided it was time they returned home. When he told Ya Beyas to prepare for the journey, Ya Beyas said no.

She said no.

And so the story goes that Pa Morlai returned to Matoko alone, where he died some years later, while Ya Beyas and her son Saidu stayed in Mamunta. It is said Ya Beyas never laid eyes on Pa Morlai again.

I don't really know if Ya Beyas and Pa Morlai's story ended that way. It's true she never went back to Matoko. Her son, Saidu, my grandfather, grew up in Mamunta and would one day be indentured by the same brothers who had redeemed

Ya Beyas. He would leave Mamunta and found a settlement of his own, which would become known as Rogbonko, the place in the forest. And on his estate indentured men would work. All of that is as Adama told it. What I am saying here is that I don't know whether the last act of defiance I like to give Ya Beyas in my retelling of the story is really true, that she looked Pa Morlai in the eye and spoke the word 'no.'

The last time I told Ya Beyas' story it was to a gathering of British people of West Indian heritage, descendants of people who had left Sierra Leone or some other African country and who when they left must have guessed that they did so without hope of return or redemption. When I came to the end of the story of my great-grandparents, to Ya Beyas' final declaration, people clapped and cheered and stamped their feet. And so I like to tell myself it really happened that way.

My aunt Adama died one year after we sat listening to her in that Freetown courtyard. She was the last member of our family who held the story of Ya Beyas and Pa Morlai. If I had not asked her to tell it to me, we would have lost it. So many things. We would have carried on thinking we were Temnes and never discovered our great-grandfather had been a Loko. The Sierra Leonians who landed in South Carolina and settled there and in Louisiana and around me here in Virginia and all over the United States brought with them only what they could carry in their memories and in their hearts. When I realised that I began to understand, in some small way, what it might feel like to lose the story of who you are.

To have it taken away from you.

In Timbuktu

In Timbuktu I stopped a man to ask him the way to the post office. The man had a question of his own that he wanted answered first. 'Is it true,' he said, 'that in Britain people have a thing about Timbuktu?'

'Yes,' I said. 'People think it is far away, like the farthest place on earth.'

At this the man laughed for a long time. Then he gave me directions to the post office.

Hame

Like birds we flew in on the breeze, landing at Aberdeen
Airport within a few minutes of each other and were reunited
at the baggage carousel. Gregor had come from Hong Kong,
where he lives and works, and I had come from the United
States, where I do the same. Our mother had arrived two days
before from Auckland, which is where she has chosen to retire,
and where she tends the orchids in her garden, attends Scottish country dancing evenings with other Scots and those of
Scottish descent and at which she wears her clan colours. Part
of her year is spent in the Scottish Highlands, in Deeside, also

a favourite destination of Britain's royal family, who summer at their royal estates nearby.

When I had first raised the idea that Gregor accompany me on a trip to the Shetlands with our mother, my brother had written back to say no. There were reasons: his wife, his son's school term. When I had written to him I hadn't imagined being joined by our families. It was to be just the three of us. Now I said to him that it was maybe the last time Mum could make such a journey. Two years earlier we had been together when Tom, my mother's husband, had died suddenly. His death, in Scotland, which had occurred on the same day as that of my father-in-law, had brought into sharp focus the fact that a generation were departing, so now I planned to avoid regrets. With fine wines and food, I added. My brother may be nearly a decade younger than me, but we are both middle-aged. Days passed and then Gregor wrote back to say he had flights held.

Our first task was a simple one: to pick up the rental car and drive the forty miles to Ballater, collect our mother and then drive back to Aberdeen's port to catch the evening ferry for the Shetland Islands. The Peugeot was black, sleek and fast. Within minutes we were driving down narrow lanes bounded by hedgerows. Apart from a brand-new commercial estate close by the terminal, there were none of the industrial wastelands and hotels that usually surround airports. Instead here were fields, cows, farmhouses and ribbons of granite bungalows.

I have written a good deal about my father, for the reason that he died when he should not have, and I have written a lot about my other country, Sierra Leone, because the last decades there have been tumultuous. Yet my earliest memories are also of Scotland, of the caravan site where, in the late 1960s, my mother lived for a year after we left Sierra Leone with her first three children (this was before Gregor, the son she would have with her second husband), and where our playmates were traveller children—gypsies, we called them back then—who came and went. My mother played guitar in a folk group and went around the pubs recording people singing old songs, and a young Rod Stewart once visited and pitched his tent outside on the grass, because there wasn't room enough for him inside our caravan. There were other days I spent at my grandparents' pebble-dash terraced house while my mother was at teacher training college, the memories of which come with the taste of my grandfather's home-grown rhubarb and of kippers eaten at their Formica kitchen table.

In the hallway of the Old Coach House sat a small suitcase next to a huge Burmese elephant chair and a shiny brass Thai noodle-sellers' cart. In the dining room, a carved and painted cabinet, also from East Asia, housed a collection of crystal glasses and decanters. Here and there lay sheepskin throws and dashes of tartan. The house has a turret and reputedly a ghost, which my mother claims to have seen. For more than half the year the house stands shuttered, empty; now the still air of the hall smelled faintly of mothballs. My mother's hair is pure silver, her eyes bird-bright. These days she looks more and more like my grandfather, though her skin wears a year-round tan I have never seen her without. By contrast, I don't remember ever seeing *him* with one.

Passing back through Ballater on our way to Aberdeen, our mother pointed out the changes to the town since we were there two years ago. Recent years have brought two disasters: the Victorian railway station burned in 2015 and then, a year later, dozens of homes were flooded when a storm caused the

River Dee to break its banks and engulf part of the town. The storm was called Frank, which is the kind of name you give to an unassuming child, or perhaps to a cat for a joke, but not a storm of such ferocity that afterwards some people decided to leave the town for good. Many of the houses displayed For Sale signs. The station had been restored, though, and now housed a replica Victorian tea room and waiting room exactly like the one used by Queen Victoria. Charles was opening another restaurant in there, my mother thought. Like all locals she refers to the royals by their first names. 'I saw Camilla driving through town the other day,' 'Kate is here again this year,' though never the Queen or the Queen Mother. Prince Charles inherited Birkhall House, a nearby 53,000-acre estate, from his grandmother, the Queen Mother, in 2002. After the floods and to help reinvigorate the town's economy, Charles opened a restaurant in Ballater, which is supplied with produce from his southerly estate at Highgrove.

Once I won a prize for a book, and with it was granted a fifteen-minute audience with the Queen. I'm told tradition dictates that visitors should not reveal the subject of conversation, but I think I can safely tell you that we talked for a short while about Deeside, which that winter had suffered record low temperatures. Minus fifteen, I remarked, as we sat side by side on a Victorian couch. The Queen murmured and then shared the observation that she had never been to Balmoral in the winter. I thought about that for a long time: to own a house you have never seen in all its seasons, and in my next book I wrote about a woman who bought a summer home in another country, one in which she had never endured winter.

There are those who leave and those who stay and there are those who come and go for some other reason: privilege, position, marriage, work, escape. In leaving Scotland and going to live overseas in the 1960s, my mother rejected the script of a life with which she had been presented and wrote her own, which is the gift she bestowed upon her children and something I only grew to understand was unusual later as, one by one, the girls with whom I had been at school retreated to the English counties and turned into their mothers. Somehow I never got that memo. My mother's children grew up in multiple countries. For me those were Scotland and Sierra Leone, later England, where I was schooled. My breaks and holidays were spent in Scotland or with my mother and step-father wherever his job had taken him: Zambia, then Iran and Thailand. My brother spent many of his early years in Thailand, before that in Iran and then, after his years attending a Scottish boarding school, went out to Hong Kong with his first job and now, in his mid-forties, is married to a woman whose own parents emigrated to Canada from China and with whom he has a son who speaks Mandarin. I came to rest in London, mostly because I went to university there and then married a Londoner, but now have spent some years at universities in America, where, for the time being at any rate, I live in Virginia close to my teaching job at Georgetown University.

In Peterculter, now an Aberdeen suburb, it is said the outlaw Rob Roy evaded capture by the Duke of Montrose's men. On a rocky outcrop stands a brightly painted statue of Rob Roy, much admired by me as a child, and in whose legendary role I often cast myself in my imaginary games. A few miles on is Gairn Terrace. My grandfather bought number 38 in the 1930s and lived there with my grandmother until her death and then his. The last time I visited the house was in

1999, months before my grandfather's death, when we drove together to Cawdor. He did not see the new century in. In early January I was back for his funeral. Apart from another time, when I took him for dinner at Banchory, I only ever saw him in the house at Gairn Terrace, though I discovered during that final visit that he had travelled far beyond the Scottish borders. That day he told me that he had become 'bored' of living and later, as we talked, showed me pictures of himself in cities and against landscapes the world over. I remember best the photo taken in Los Angeles with the Hollywood sign in the hills behind him, and another of him standing at the lip of the Grand Canyon, dressed in pleated slacks and short-sleeved shirt—when I had never seen him in anything other than tweeds—a leather camera case dangling from his neck. We, his grandchildren, used to joke that Grandad, who wore a thin moustache and his hair swept back, looked like the actor Lawrence Olivier playing a Nazi, and the images he showed me that day, because I'd never seen him go anywhere, looked as if they had been taken by a prankster with a cardboard cut-out. Grandad had worked for many years doing the accounts for a travel agency. A job, he told me, that came with the benefit of discounted travel.

My grandfather, Robert Christison, was born in the grounds of Holyrood Park in Edinburgh, where his father was a gamekeeper. His family were migrants from Unst in the Shetland Islands, which is where we were headed that day in late May of 2019. To travel to the Shetlands may be the closest one can come nowadays to travel as it might have been before the era of commercial jetliners. There are flights, but they are expensive and so most people take the ferry, which leaves Aberdeen harbour in the evening and makes a late stop at

Kirkwall in the Orkneys before steaming north-east through
the night to Lerwick in the Shetlands, arriving at seven the
next morning.

Aboard the *Hrossey*, islanders easily outnumbered tourists.
Our cabins came with bathrooms and a sea view. In the dining
room we sat down to a three-course dinner and watched the
pilot boat drop back, like a pacesetter leaving a runner to close
the race. The ferry surged onward, and the sea walls of old
Aberdeen slipped away. There were wind turbines, burn-off
stacks, research vessels heavy with equipment; a gull hovered
at the window, disappeared and hove back into view a few
seconds later. We had a sighting of a dolphin or perhaps it
was a porpoise. The metallic waters of the North Sea were
slick and still.

Gregor was pleased. Pleased by the view, pleased by the
haddock chowder, the comparative luxury of the Magnus
Lounge's wood panelling and leather seats, pleased by the
wine he and I were drinking. Our mother never drinks, but
she too was pleased, if less exuberantly so, for she was what
had brought us together. Apart from the fact that she is our
mother and the person who binds us to Scotland, she was the
reason for this trip. In recent years, and in the way of retired
folk, she has made a pastime of genealogy. My mother was not
the first in her family to leave the place where she was born,
although that's how it always seemed. Well before her own
departure, family members had drifted outward to Australia, South Africa, Canada, the United States and beyond. As
populations become ever more fluid making family ties more
tenuous, people search for other forms of continuity to replace
the land to which we were once bound. On the restaurant
table my mother laid maps, charts and guidebooks. I became

lost—and not for the last time—in the labyrinth of births, deaths and marriages she has mapped. What I noticed, as she spoke, was her description of the journeys undertaken by these long-dead folk. This one left for the Mainland. That one went to Australia. This one was lost at sea. For my mother the act of tracing her ancestors has seemed to be as much about finding out where and who she came from, as discovering the pioneering spirit of those who went before. Gregor swirled his wine in his glass, looked over the rim at the map and said cheerfully: 'So, where are we going, anyway?'

We were going as far north as it is possible to go and still be on the British Isles. From Lerwick we would drive up the island, take another ferry to Yell, on the far side of Yell we would catch the ferry to Unst, drive for another forty minutes until we arrived in Haroldswick, the most northerly settlement in the British Isles, three hundred miles from Aberdeen and eight hundred miles from London. The Shetlands are a sub-Arctic archipelago of Scotland, repeatedly plundered and finally settled by Vikings who ruled for six hundred years and used the Shetlands and Orkneys as a base for their raids. After a failed rebellion by the ruling Viking earl, Norway brought the islands back under direct rule, which it maintained until 1469, when the king of Norway, Denmark and Sweden offered the islands in surety against the dowry of his daughter Margaret, then betrothed to James III of Scotland. The dowry never was paid. Scotland has retained the Shetlands ever since.

May to July in the Shetlands is the Simmer Dim, when day stretches into night and the sun barely drops below the horizon. At this time of year it is light for nineteen hours of the day. After dinner Gregor told a story of visiting Svalbard in the Arctic after hearing about the famous Polar Summer.

They were three friends from Hong Kong; Gregor was charged with organising the trip. They travelled north only to arrive in a darkness that never eased. He had booked for the wrong time of year. They toured the town and saw nothing. One, a former banker from Sri Lanka, had in his suitcase three pairs of designer sunglasses, which he sported anyway.

In the Shetlands, at this time of year, tourists come for two reasons. There are the twitchers, for the islands are renowned for their birdlife, puffins in particular, and many other varieties of seabird: guillemots, kittiwakes, razorbills and gannet, which nest in breeding grounds on the islands' cliffs. The other kind of tourist, people like us, are here in search of the past.

Early the next morning, I drew back the blackout curtain of the cabin I shared with my mother to a view of the cliffs at the southerly tip of the Shetland Mainland. Less than an hour after docking and driving the length of the island, a much smaller ferry carried us to Yell, an island made of peat, like a big peat patty, on which the most common activity (after fishing and fish farming) is, unsurprisingly, peat harvesting. At the other end of Yell we arrived to find the first ferry to Unst full and so we went to the ticket office to book ourselves onto the next available crossing. We had paid for a return ticket, but once aboard, the ferryman took our ticket but failed to return the stub. On the Shetlands you show your ticket on the way north but nobody bothers you for it on the way south: 'For how else did you get there in the first place?' said the ferryman.

Haroldswick, so named for the Viking king Harald, of the famous Icelandic chronicle *Haralds saga Sigurðarsonar*, which tells of his exploits, romantic, military and religious in Sicily, Palestine, Jerusalem and Novgorod. Haroldswick is reputed to be the first place in the British Isles the Vikings disembarked from their longships and where they came to settle. There's a reconstruction of a longship on the road into the hamlet. Longships were capable of carrying one hundred people as well as their animals. For several centuries the Vikings occupied themselves with raids on settlements as far north as Iceland and Greenland, south to Andalusia and the North African Coast, east to the Black and Caspian Seas and, at least once, west to Newfoundland. They guided their longships by the sun and stars and followed the migratory flight path of birds.

Most everyone on Unst has Viking, or at least Norse, blood. According to DNA test results, I carry two per cent Norwegian blood. This puts me in the company of the nearly thirty per cent of Shetlanders who carry Norse DNA. My grandfather's last name was Christison, the distinctly Scandinavian 'son of Christian.' 'We're descended from Vikings,' my mother had told the ferryman on the way over, to which he had replied, 'Aren't we all?'

Alongside my DNA results, the company I used provided migratory maps of my ancestors, which showed other elements of my Scots family arriving in the Shetlands from the Highlands sometime between 1775 and 1800, around the time of the Highland Clearances. Thousands of families were evicted from their homes by wealthy landowners who wished to use the land for raising sheep. Many went to Canada and Australia, but more on that later. At least one part of my grandfather's family travelled in the opposite direction, shipping out to the islands, to the Orkneys and Shetlands.

The Arctic winds that blow across the Shetlands flatten everything in their path, leaving a landscape that is stark and treeless. We passed a single stand of trees, enclosed by stone walls, that had grown their crowns all bent in the same direction, like a crowd of old men holding up broken umbrellas. Though it was halfway through May, their branches were bare. The winter winds reach seventy miles an hour. Life survives by hugging the earth: tiny Shetland ponies and Highland cattle. The first time I visited the Shetlands was in 2010 when I had gone there with my husband. I had been giving a talk at Aberdeen University and decided to stay and visit with my mother, but she hadn't arrived yet from New Zealand, and so we filled the time by travelling to the islands. We had met a chocolatier on Unst, who with his wife had decided the next turn in their lives with eyes closed. Thus they had stuck a pin in a map. The pin landed in Wales and so they went online and bought a house there, sight unseen, and which, through error, either in the description or misreading on their part, turned out to be in the Shetlands. Still, they pressed on, relocated and began shipping raw chocolate to the islands where they opened a chocolaterie, Britain's 'most northerly' (which visitors soon discover is a description applied to almost every retail opportunity in Unst). The chocolatier had described for us the shock of the winters, the hours spent setting rat traps around the outside walls of their house to stop the animals from gnawing their way inside.

'They're gone,' said the ferry pilot, when Gregor and I visited the pilothouse and I asked if the chocolate shop was still there. We told him we were here to see the croft our ancestors had once farmed on Unst, to which he had replied: 'Which one?' We were caught out by the unexpectedness of the question, also we hadn't been paying proper attention to our mother's charts and maps the evening before, thus we failed in our reply. Instead we learned that Shetlanders, those who stay, know where they came from with pinpoint precision. Feall is marked on maps of Unst and signposted on the road and it took us no time at all to find. Feall, it turned out, comprised three properties, two ruined croft houses and one that looked like a new build, which my mother figured to have been raised on the site of a third croft. In one of these had lived Ursula Cecilia Heinrickson, my great-great-grandmother.

I untied the knot on the gate, and we crossed the field towards the nearest ruin. Ahead of us a whimbrel shot from the undergrowth. The building's stonework had withstood time well, the main structures and supporting walls were in place, including the door and window lintels. Among the stones I found old bottles, the glass heavy and clouded, and a Vaseline petroleum jelly jar from the 1930s. By the gate of the second croft house lay a dead lamb, its eyes pecked out. Birds nested in the alcoves of the ruins. Crofters survived on whatever they could grow or forage from the land and take from the sea. They raised animals and grew what vegetables they could: the men fished, the young women worked as 'gutter girls,' hands deep in herring innards at the fishery, the old women knitted fine, woollen shawls. The 1886 Crofting Act offered some tenancy protections, but in Ursula's time the crofters were entirely beholden to the landlords to whom they paid dues, in their case the Earl of Zetland. In time Ursula Heinrickson left the island and, somewhere along the way, dropped Ursula in favour of Cecilia and changed Heinrickson to Henderson, and as Cecilia Henderson she took a job serving table in a large house in Edinburgh.

'I question if it was ever a viable livelihood,' said Robert Hughson, whom I met and talked to at the hotel bar while I

waited for my mother to come down from her room. Robert
had crofted, worked as a lighthouse attendant, sold insur-
ance, tried and failed to grow trees. Spruce from Norway and
lodgepole pine, he told me; the seeds for the latter he sourced
and had sent from Vancouver Island, but even they could not
withstand the 'salt blast.' For those who stay, life shares one
thing with the crofters: they do what it takes to survive. In
The Prairie in Her Eyes, Ann Daum writes of her hometown
of Murdo in South Dakota: 'Don't ask me how people know.
I knew. I could run a finger down the pictures in the high
school yearbook, picking out who would stay and who would
go.' Like Unst, Murdo is also a place where the wind blows
hard all year long.

Robert's grandfather John, or Auld Erin, had been a sixareen skipper in the late 1800s. Robert's son had joined the
outflow of islanders and lived now in New Zealand. Robert's
daughter, on the other hand, was a stayer like her father and
taught junior high to the islands' fifty children who, in order
to attend sixth form, must leave for Lerwick or Brae, forty
and sixty miles away on the main island.

Depopulation has been a concern in the Shetlands for more
than half a century. In 1960 Shetlanders came up with the idea
for a Hamefarin, a festival conceived as a way of reconnecting
with kinfolk the world over, of letting them know they were
always welcome back. Roughly a thousand descendants of
Shetlanders—*hamefarers*—from all over the world travelled
to the islands for the last Hamefarin in 2010, among them
my mother.

'It's funny you came to write about stayers, but actually
everyone leaves,' remarked Gregor a day into the trip. That was
the thought that had begun our journey, which we'd talked

about on the ferry over when I'd said that although we lived at a time when public and media attention was focussed on those who migrated, I was interested in what it was that compelled people to stay in the place they first called home, or *hame*. Ideas of home produce a cultural schism, for home is at once the focus of great nostalgia for some, equally for others home is a place they can't wait to get away from. Home is somewhere you escape from, grow out of, return to. Yet even those who revere the idea of home rarely seem able adequately to describe it. I am often asked the question, Where is home? and sense that my efforts at a reply are found wanting. The reason for this, I believe, is a conceptual mismatch between me and my interlocutor on the definition of the word home. For them, those people who want an answer from me, I have discovered two things to be consistently true: home is always located in the past. It is not enough for me to say, 'Arlington.' Also, it is a noun used strictly in the singular. The word 'homes' is antithetical to the idea of home.

I am someone who can live (within reason) anywhere. So is my mother and so is my brother. Joan Didion, who is seven years older than my mother, wrote in her 1967 essay, 'On Going Home': 'Sometimes I think that those of us who are now in our thirties were born into the last generation to carry the burden of "home."' I don't suppose my mother read Didion's essay, though she is the embodiment of it, the most itinerant person I have ever known. My mother has lived in nineteen countries on five continents, first with one husband and then another and then alone. In between she has visited dozens more, taking in new countries year by year. She has travelled with a husband and small children, she has travelled alone, by plane, train and automobile and on foot, often to places considered unsafe. Now, frustrated by the constraints of age, she has accepted the necessity of travelling companions and will board a coach or a cruise ship, though she remains resolute in her need to leave home. When I think of this need in her, I realise I should have been unsurprised by my grandfather's trove of travel pictures. As for me, I have to travel so often for work that I have come to regard staying home as a luxury. Also, I am something of a homebody; it is simply that I am flexible about where exactly that home might be.

To the woman in attendance at the heritage museum, my mother explained we came from several generations of Shetlanders, but that now she lived mainly in New Zealand. 'I think it's the Viking in me,' she said. The attendant had welcomed us with a smile of superior warmth and was full of vim, producing an island narrative so seamless and tailored ('Your ancestors would have knitted shawls like these, worn shoes like these, cooked with this . . .') that she might have been an actor. In fact, 'The Actress' is how we referred to her from then on. The Shetland tourist season lasts just six weeks and so the welcome, unlike the weather, barely has time to cool.

The Actress showed my mother and brother a map on the wall and invited us to stick a pin in the place where we came from. I stuck a pin in Virginia, though it could equally have been London, where I have lived since I was eighteen and my husband and I own our one and only house. And then I stuck one in Sierra Leone, because nobody else had done so. My brother pushed his into Hong Kong and my mother tried to find a space near Auckland, which bristled with pins. In the Shetlands, many of the assumptions I had become used to hearing about race and migration were altered. On these remote islands there was an acceptance that everyone came from some-where else and that people often did not stay put. It changed the air, made it fresher and purer. The question 'Where do you come from?' is not followed by the spoken or silent 'originally,' but the word 'now.' The Shetlands, whose official website states: 'We offer a safe and welcoming haven for people from all walks of life,' is one of the few places in the world currently encour-aging immigrants. Apparently, Svalbard is another. That night I thought about my mother's restless spirit, which I have grown up with and always taken for granted and wondered if it came to her channelled through the thwarted dreams of her father or whether it really could be because once we were Vikings. By that I mean that the idea that life is meant to be lived in one place is not part of our cultural memory as it is in the ancestral narratives of certain other people.

My grandfather's relatives left their homelands in droves. Four went to Australia. Shetlanders were prized for their sea-faring skills and one became the chief pilot in Sydney har-bour and owned land at Vaucluse, now called Christison Park. Three brothers started a sheep station in Lammermoor outside Brisbane, one was washed away with his horse, attempting to cross a river in spate. A second turned humanitarian, cam-paigning on behalf of aboriginal peoples displaced by farmers like him. His daughter, Mary Bennette, wrote a monograph on him, *Robert Christison of Lammermoor*. After his death Mary pursued Robert's work and later published *Hunt and Die: The Prospect for the Aborigines of Australia*, a pamphlet for the London Anti-Slavery Society. Two other Christisons became missionaries. One is buried in Uganda (meaning my mother was not the first in her family to leave Scotland for Africa, though perhaps she was the first woman), the other drowned when his ship was attacked by pirates in the South China Sea. Several Christisons joined the army and fought in India and Burma, of which the best known, Major General Alexander Frank Philip Christison, fought in both world wars, rose through various overseas commands, finally to take the Japanese surrender in Singapore on September 3, 1945. He died at the age of a hundred back in Scotland and the *New York Times* carried his obituary. My mother recounts these stories over huge wedges of cake in a tea shop, Britain's north-ernmost, naturally. Ordinarily, I don't care much for cake, but this cream-and-jam-filled sponge struck me as uncommonly delicious. I ate it all, as though I were someone else.

Lydia Margaret Jean Bruce Duncan, my grandmother, was the only person I have ever known to emigrate and fail, though I am sure it happens. In those days there was such a thing as 'assisted emigration,' under the Empire Settlement Act, which grew out of the British desire for colonial expansion. Two uncles and an aunt had already left for Toronto. Lydia's mother, my great-grandmother Maggie Jean, stayed in Scotland. Maggie Jean's husband, Alfred, was paraplegic. A prizewinning swimmer, he had dived off the Old Bridge of Dee to save a friend who had leapt into the water and was pretending to be in difficulties. This followed an afternoon of drinking. The water, it turned out, was only a few feet deep. Alfred broke his back and was crippled. The nurse who cared for him was Maggie Jean, whom he later married. Alfred died before I was born. Of Maggie Jean all I remember is her great musquash coat. Maggie's brothers, Charles and James, and sister, Bella, left for Canada. In time Lydia followed her uncles and aunt, where she found work as a shopgirl, employed by the Hudson's Bay Trading Company in Toronto.

There is a photograph of Lydia in Canada, the only hard evidence she was ever there. She sits on a beach, wearing a bathing costume, her bobbed hair worn in a loose wave and parted in the centre. My mother, showing me the photograph for the first time, pointed out that the people behind Lydia were all fully dressed. There is a woman wearing a heavy winter hat and a coat, the hemline of which drops to a few inches above her ankle. Lydia's hair and her black bathing costume belong to the 1920s; she was born in 1909 and she looks around sixteen so this would place the date of the picture at, maybe, 1925. That year *Mrs Dalloway* and *The Great Gatsby* were published, the bus carrying Frida Kahlo hit a streetcar, in Italy Mussolini suspended democracy and, in an event that likely went unreported, Hitler published *Mein Kampf.* It was also the era of female emancipation. Lydia had gone to Canada, she had cut her hair and here she is, smiling a little uncertainly as she models swimwear for the Hudson's Bay Trading Company summer catalogue on a beach in winter. Within two years of the photograph she would be back in Aberdeen. She waited until the day the mandatory period of residency in Canada was over in order to avoid repaying her outward passage, and then she caught a steamer back to Scotland. She would never return, not even when Bella bequeathed to her a house in Toronto. Maggie Jean made the journey in her daughter's stead and sold the house. Lydia is said to have been ill with meningitis during her Toronto years, but had made a full recovery. My mother said Lydia spoke only Doric and no English at the time, that perhaps she had trouble fitting in, but between us we decided that wouldn't have mattered, given the numbers of Scots resettling in Canada. Did something else happen? Did she ever talk about it? asked my brother. Not really, said my mother. My grandfather, the once I spoke to him about Lydia's time in Canada during my last visit to Gairn Terrace, said: 'I reckon your grandmother became homesick.'

Given the mark human migration has made on the modern world, you'd think psychologists would have investigated the phenomenon of homesickness more thoroughly, but as yet no clear definition has even been agreed. In 1688, a Swiss medical student, Johannes Hofer, coined the term nostalgia— *nostos* (for 'returning home') and *algia* (for 'pain')—to describe homesickness, a mental illness which manifested itself in physical pain. Hofer had observed the case of a student who suffered anxiety attacks, loss of appetite and sleeplessness, but who recovered once he was sent home—to die, doctors had thought. Nowadays 'nostalgia' refers to a yearning for a lost past, something that many of us feel. Not everyone leaves the place where they grew up, but we can all wistfully recall a time when we were younger or fitter or carefree, or someone we loved was alive.

'Do you get homesick?' I asked my brother. He shook his head. Neither do I. But then, boarding school will do that for you. We all got homesick in those first years: quietly sobbing in the darkness of the dormitory. Then, after a long summer at home, we'd grow bored and yearn for our friends and the routine of classes, prep and sports, only to miss home again. Strictly, though, it was my parents I missed, for we often spent each holiday in a different country. Wherever they were, I felt safe. Perhaps I had already lost my attachment to place. There were children who never stopped weeping and who, after a few weeks or sometimes a term or two, would be quietly removed. At some point, though, even those children would grow up and presumably leave home, severing the bond to place.

When we move town or country, we may miss our favourite foods, walks and shops. In America I developed a longing for Scotch egg and kippers. And then there are the intangible things: the ease of a long friendship, the subtle codes of behaviour and language that my subconscious does the work of detecting. When I return to London from the United States, I feel the relaxing of a guard I hadn't realised was there. I am pleased to be in a place I know, but it is not a requirement for my happiness. Some people are more home-struck than others. There are people who, I suppose, must find my way of being as impossible to imagine as I find what seems to me to be an excessive need for the familiar. I worry faintly for these people. I think, what if some great change were wrought upon them? War, perhaps. How would they cope?

People who, as adults, seem unable to stop feeling homesick are, according to the research, typically those with dependency or attachment issues: meaning they are *insecurely* attached, or else in the grip of some psychopathology, depression or agoraphobia, for instance. Maybe the idea of making a new life demanded too much of Lydia, maybe Toronto made Lydia feel unsafe. Maybe in order to feel safe, she needed a familiar script, one she knew and understood.

In her later years I cannot recall my grandmother ever leaving 38 Gairn Terrace. I have a very early memory of her taking me to the park when I was three or four, and there are photographs of her with my elder brother, sister and me when we were very little in Deeside, so she ventured those few miles, at least. All the time my grandfather was travelling, she stayed at home. Once, in my late teens, we took her to Banchory for lunch. We waited in the sitting room while Gran got ready and when, finally, she came downstairs and saw the breakfast dishes had not been done she became agitated, pulled off her gloves and unpinned her hat and would not get into the car until they were washed and dried. My mother was displeased with my stepfather who had been reading a newspaper instead of helping. Her own energy was focussed on willing my grand-mother out of the house, and soon mine was too. I sensed that if we let Gran turn back again for any reason, the whole endeavour would be lost. That was in the early 1980s. I never saw her leave the house again, not even to go to the shops. All her groceries were delivered, her 'messages' as she called them, orders from the fishmonger and the butcher whose vans stopped outside the house every Friday.

Later that day on Unst, the three of us walked on Norwick Beach, where water, sand and sky comprised shifting shades of silver and grey. On the beach I photographed the corpses of seabirds. There was one, a tern perhaps, mostly down to bones, though its wings and flight feathers had remained intact and it lay outspread upon the sand, like the skeleton of an angel. There was a gannet, of which there are only four breeding colonies on the Shetland cliffs. When gannets fish they fold their wings, which have a near six-feet span, and hit the water with such speed that their bodies have adapted to withstand the force by developing air sacs in the chest and head to protect them from damage. And yet here was one of nature's greatest divers, apparently drowned.

The seas were still that day, but are frequently implacable. In Ursula's time, the men drowned a half dozen at a time when their sixareens foundered and capsized. The boats put out for days, sometimes venturing forty miles from shore where the fish hauls were richer; in this they outstripped the yoals, the other kind of fishing boat Shetlanders used, which were not built for the deeper waters. Hands blistered by the oars and cut by the lines, of which they might set up to six miles a day and which took four or five hours to haul in, the men remained at their posts throughout, exposed to the wind, salt and cold. In these waters off Norwick Beach, one day or night in 1869, drowned Henry Henderson, age forty-five. To the bottom of the sea Henry followed his father, also Henry, and elder brother Lawrence who had perished together twelve years before. The men were my fourth and fifth great-uncles. The descendants of these men left the islands, their crofts stand ruined and the last sixareen set sail for the final time only a few decades after they left.

The next day we caught the ferry to Orkney, disembarked close to midnight and drove the forty minutes to our hotel at speed through a dark so deep it might have been solid. From the back my mother wondered aloud if we shouldn't slow down. 'Don't worry,' I said. I was perfectly relaxed. 'Greg can fly a helicopter,' which is true. It's something he does. And my mother replied: 'This isn't a helicopter.'

The Orkney archipelago lies ten miles north of mainland Scotland and is made up of seventy islands and skerries, fifty of which are uninhabited. We were headed to South Ronald-say, one of the south islands, which is linked to the mainland and the islands of Burray, Lamb Holm and Glimps Holm by a series of Churchill Barriers. My phone reception proved too variable to rely on satellite navigation and so I directed Gregor as best I could, by counting the number of barriers we crossed. Gregor knew his military history and described how the barriers were ordered to be built by Winston Churchill after a German U-boat, in one of the most daring wartime attacks ever recorded, navigated its way through submarine nets and sunken 'block' ships to torpedo the HMS *Royal Oak*, then anchored in the natural—and until then presumed unbreachable—harbour of Scapa Flow.

We had spent our night on Unst at the disused RAF airbase of Saxa Vord, sleeping on bunks in the unconverted quarters. Gregor and I set our alarms early, planning to walk the cliffs in the hope of spotting some puffins. I'd seen hundreds of them there on my last trip, but in the intervening years the puffins have begun to vanish. On the Shetlands their numbers and those of all migratory seabirds have plunged precipitously. Researchers blame climate change for causing an increase in sea and air temperatures in the North and North Atlantic Sea, disrupting food chains on which the migrating birds rely.

At dawn I'd woken to the sound of pouring rain. Outside a heavy fog had reduced visibility to fifty yards or so. I dressed anyway and knocked on Gregor's door. We decided that rather than waste the effort we had already made in rising, we would go for a drive. As we passed the turnoff to the cliffs, I felt a nip of disappointment. Seeing the puffins had been the high point of my last visit, for you don't have to be a bird enthusiast to be enthralled by these remarkable-looking clown birds or sea parrots, as they are sometimes called. We wound up at the Cold War–era RAF radar station at the tip of the island. The sentry posts were abandoned, and much of the fencing and the signs were rusted. One, warning against unauthorised personnel, however, definitely looked new to me and an interior gate bore a shining padlock and chain. During the Cold War, the Soviet Union regularly tested NATO's northern air and sea defences with the aim, it was believed, of positioning a nuclear submarine within striking range of the United States.

Today the station has come back into operation in response to concerns about the global ambitions of Vladimir Putin.

On Orkney, the Churchill Barriers have been converted into narrow, spray-soaked causeways, which link the Mainland and Burray as well as the two small islands, on one of which stands the so-called Italian Chapel, built by the wartime prisoners who were forced to work on constructing the barriers in breach of international law. The causeways are unlit, the hulls of scuttled battleships loom out of the water, which is a mere feet away; in rough weather they become impassable.

St Margaret's Hope is an attractive seaside town on the island of South Ronaldsay. In the morning and after two days in the car, Gregor and I felt the need for exercise and went for a run. 'Here comes the city,' I said, imagining how we must look to an older man with a newspaper, getting out of his car. 'Where did you say you were from, again. Hong Kong, is it?' Gregor dialled up his own, now much softened, Scottish accent. 'Well, why don't you fuck off back there?' The accent I had in the first few years of my life and when I was pretty much just learning to speak is long gone, except for when I say two words, which I never noticed until my husband pointed it out. I say 'wurrald' for world and 'tuth' not tooth. My mother's accent has remained intact through five decades abroad in an act, I have come to believe, of sheer will. 'Good morning!' we called as we drew parallel to the man, and if the sight of us struck him in any way curious, he only nodded and replied in kind.

In daylight it became apparent how different the Orkney Islands are from the Shetlands. Beneath the shadow of the clouds the land shone with dew and glimmered green. Here it seemed as if everything grew in abundance. We passed

field after field of cattle, fat as Apollonian herds, each one
comprising a bull, several cows and many calves, who trotted
over to form an orderly semicircle around us when we stopped
for breath.

Here on Orkney once lived more of our grandfather's relatives whose genealogical lines would eventually intersect with
the Shetlanders. Donald Sutherland, a wealthy farmer, owned
three properties in these parts: Sutherland, Pole and Skerpie,
all of which are still farmed.

Donald's daughter, Elizabeth, married a man called
John Budge. After the marriage Sutherland made Budge his
farm manager. Elizabeth, though, was dead at twenty-nine.
Sutherland erected a memorial to Elizabeth, her sister who
had died three years earlier at the age of twenty and their
mother, Helen Copland, at the nearby graveyard of St Lawrence's. Elizabeth and John's son, James, left the islands for
Edinburgh, where he met and married a young woman who
had also come from the islands, from Unst, and who was
serving table in a private house—Ursula Heinrickson, who
now called herself Cecilia Henderson. Cecilia and James were
my great-great-grandparents.

St Lawrence's on the north-eastern shore of Burray Island
sits in isolation above a scimitar of blue bay. There stand the
ruins of a small chapel and a walled, treeless graveyard. The
graveyard and chapel seemed caught in the nexus of sea, sky
and land and I remember that it struck me as a beautiful place
to worship, but also one created to test the faithful, for it lay
at the end of a long, unsheltered road, and there would have
been no way to reach it except on foot or by horse and trap
and the chapel seemed deliberately positioned to take the force
of the sea gales. The gravestones were covered in pale lichen

of a semi-luminous green, which grew thick like grass, and dark moss obscured much of their lettering. On the ground lay the hollow shell of a gull's egg.

I remember the keenness of the air that afternoon, how we walked with our shoulders up around our chins and how I tried to protect my ears by covering them with my hands. The gravestones bearing the names of Elizabeth, Catherine and Helen stood against one of the chapel walls. 'Here are your ancestors,' my mother said, repeating herself again twice more. But I felt nothing except the freezing cold. True, in those carved letters we were looking at the only real evidence of an existence, for in the Shetlands every one of our ancestors had either left to die elsewhere or lay on the seabed.

The next day was our last; it was also Gregor's birthday. In London, Theresa May resigned as prime minister over Brexit, though nobody we met mentioned it. In Hong Kong there were protests. Gregor called his family and we talked and watched each other through a screen and across countless miles. Later we visited neolithic sites, which in Orkney are scattered across the landscape, much the way I remember being astonished at first to see ancient ruins in Greece or Turkey, lying on the outskirts of a town or half hidden in a tangle of overgrowth on a coastal road. Sheep grazed beneath the Standing Stones of Stenness, a henge of megaliths each six metres high, and at the Ring of Brodgar, birds nested in the stonewalls of the settlement at Skarra Brae. We visited the Tomb of the Eagles and Maeshowe, a burial chamber older than the pyramids of Egypt, and which in the twelfth century had once been looted by a Viking earl whose men left the walls covered in graffiti. Many of the sites were within minutes of each other and we drove guided by Bruce, as we had come to call the GPS voice, who pronounced the local names with his own Australian inflection. Starting route to *Mash-ow*. Starting route to *Brod-ja*. In the evening and on our way to dinner at a country hotel, Bruce got lost and directed us into the driveway of a suburban home on the far side of a tall hedge, on the other side of which was the hotel where we had a table booked for dinner. Is he drunk? someone said. 'It's just through the hedge. Nearly there. Good luck, mate,' said Gregor in an Australian accent, which he was still using when he stopped to ask directions from a passerby, and when I teased him for it, he told me that his accent had always been 'pliable.' Gregor is one of those people who unconsciously imitates the accent of whomever they're talking to. So is my mother.

The inside of the hotel looked like an antique dealer's warehouse; a proliferation of sofas and occasional tables filled the lounge. We sat by a window and I drank a gin and tonic. At dinner there was good wine, local scallops and beef. We were all in excellent humour. In the final hours of the day we had headed to the Brough of Birsay, arriving at exactly the right time for the tide to allow us to walk the causeway to the island. Gregor and I made the climb up to the top of the cliffs, purposefully heading in the opposite direction to the few other walkers. There was a lighthouse bearing a brass plaque to the memory of an airman who had died on that very day some years before. And there were seabirds in their thousands, wheeling and crying in the air. At the sight of the cliff edge my head swam with vertigo. I dropped to my knees, crawled a short distance and then fell on my face, while Gregor continued the advance. From time to time I lifted my head and scanned for puffins.

When I first visited the islands, I had thought puffins were about the size of penguins and was surprised to find them not much bigger than my hand. Apparently, this is a common mistake. The inclination to think puffins are bigger than they are has to do, I imagine, with the little birds' upright bearing, their horizon-scanning gaze. In flight, their small, rapidly beating wings make puffins look like clockwork toys. The first puffin I saw was just coming into land. Twenty minutes or so later Gregor spotted a nesting pair and handed me the binoculars where I lay on the grass. Just three puffins.

War, wildfire, weather, catastrophic or simply seasonal— humans roam for many reasons, which may be earthly or spiritual. The DNA test I had taken on a whim a while back had revealed something else. I am not, at least not in genetic terms, from Sierra Leone at all, but from Mali. Almost fifty per cent of my DNA comes from a country whose lands embrace savannah, Sahel and Sahara. This finding corresponds with the oral history of my father's side of the family, which says that the first Fornas to arrive in Sierra Leone were Muslim horsemen who had galloped down from the north carrying the word of the Prophet. When I told my sister we were Malian, she said: 'Isn't Mali one of your favourite countries?' This is true. Also I like horses a great deal. The other truth, however, is that Mali is a beautiful country and millions of people love horses. There was romance, though, in the dream of the 'once upon a time.'

In her garden at the Old Coach House, my mother puts out raisins for the blackbirds, the robins and the starlings, bird breeds which typically overwinter in Scotland and are notoriously territorial but will also migrate if temperatures drop too low or food sources become scarce. Twelve thousand years ago human beings settled and farmed and felt the need to defend what they had claimed for themselves from the claims of others. And so they started to tell stories, stories that staked their rights to the place they lived and tied their sons and daughters to the soil. People talk about roots, but plants have roots not human beings. Humans have feet and feet are meant for walking. When the Vikings learned to build boats, they climbed into those and sailed the seas. Now that we can fly, we have become birds.

And some people are robins and blackbirds and others of us are guillemots, kittiwakes and puffins.

How Stories Get Told

Kenya, 2008. I'd been in the country for a literary festival and workshop teaching young Kenyan writers and, by a piece of good fortune, was offered a commission by a glossy magazine that took me into a world I had only ever seen on television. I had a vehicle, driver and guide, Senteu, a knowledgeable and remarkably young Masai. On one of our first game drives we passed an antelope herd crowded in and around a stand of trees. Hundreds of animals. From what I could see they were all fully grown and bore antlers. A short way from the grove several were jousting and locking horns, in a fight that seemed somewhere beyond playful, but short of serious. I pointed them out to my guide, and he waved for the driver to stop.

'That's the bachelor herd,' said Senteu. He explained that these were the males who had failed to attract females, so they formed a separate herd. When I was a child, I loved watching wildlife programmes and I'd sometimes asked myself the question, If one male serviced a herd of females, what happened to the other males? We watched the bachelor herd for a while as they grazed and made dummy charges at each other. Senteu said this was likely a good place to see lions, as the lionesses frequently hunted at the edges of the herd. Occupied with competing with each other, the young bucks tended to be less watchful compared to females with young, who were constantly alert to any danger. 'That's not what you see on the wildlife programmes,' I said.

He smiled: 'They always show the young being caught, yes?' And went on to explain how comparatively rare such an event was. 'So, you're saying that lionesses feed their cubs on the carcasses of beta males?' And again, Senteu smiled.

The Last Vet

First you notice the dogs. In all other ways Freetown is a West African city like any other, of red dust and raised cries, forty-degree heat and a year neatly segmented into two—hot and dry, hot and wet.

Today water tips from the sky. Beneath the canopy of a local store three street dogs and a man holding a briefcase stand and contemplate the rain. Another dog shelters beneath the umbrella of a cigarette seller. A fifth follows a woman across the street, literally dogging her footsteps, using her as a beacon to navigate the traffic and the floodwater.

In the dry season the kings of the city are the dogs. They weave through the crowds, lie in the roadside shade watching through slitted eyes, they circle and squabble and unite in the occasional frenzied dash. For the most part the people and the dogs exist on separate planes. The dogs ignore the people, who likewise step around and over them. On the road the drivers steer around reclining animals. This city has more street dogs than any I have known.

It is eight o'clock on a Wednesday morning. Torrents of water sluice off the hills and rush down the cross streets. The force of the rain has swept the traffic off the road, and now threatens the battered Peugeot ahead of me. Inside his clinic Dr Jalloh has placed his plans on hold, waits for me in his tiny surgery surrounded by dogs, waits for the rain to stop. The whole city waits for the rain to stop.

It was the dry season of 2004 and I was home working on a novel when I first met Gudush Jalloh. My friend Rosa called, concerned that her dog, at that moment whelping, was in trouble. The dog was a snappish bitch, a street rescue by the name of Corre whom I had so far failed to befriend. I was in that selfish space of writers and the interruption was unwelcome. Could she not call a vet? She told me the vet was upcountry. Call another vet? There was no other vet. Someone who knows about dogs, then? Yes, she replied, and waited for my answer.

I know a bit about dogs. I do not pretend to know a great deal. I enjoy the company of dogs and keep them but know nothing of whelping bitches. I consider myself something less than an expert. An interested amateur.

*   *   *

Eyes closed, half in, half out of this world, the puppy looked dead. I had no idea what to do so I telephoned my husband in South East London, who in turn called our vet and relayed his instructions via mobile phone and satellite to reach us six thousand miles away, at a pound a minute. Try to free the pup's shoulders. Olive oil might help. Corre, by now docile in her distress, allowed me to try to hook my forefingers under the puppy's forelegs. I tried. Nothing worked: not the olive oil, the bitch's efforts, or my own fumblings. At last we obtained the home number of the local vet. He'd travelled overnight from the Provinces, been asleep less than an hour and his telephone manner displayed the lagged thinking of the abruptly awoken. He told me he had sent his car away. I offered to collect him.

Dr Jalloh is the only vet in the country. No, that is not quite true. There are three government vets, employed by the Ministry of Agriculture. They wear rubber boots but mostly deal with figures, with capacities, stock and yields. There are also a small number of charlatans. Gudush Jalloh is the only qualified vet in private practice. The single person in the country to whom you might bring your sick dog, cat, monkey or goat.

The pup had never, not for an instant, known life. The body cavity was a huge fluid-filled sac, devoid of vital organs. By now we had moved Corre to the surgery. Dr Jalloh prodded at the dead puppy with a long pair of tweezers and declared this the second instance of such abnormality he had seen. Rosa turned away. I, whose paper-mask fantasies had never found expression, leaned in. A second pup suffered the same deformity. Another was stillborn. Four survived.

That first meeting made a deep impression upon me. In the years that followed I met Gudush Jalloh on one more occasion which was significant, and then socially perhaps five or six times more. At one point somebody mentioned his work with the street dogs, in which they thought I might be interested.

In the 1970s, growing up in Freetown, I gathered, rescued, raised and lost more dogs than I can now recall. I have some of their names: Jack, Jim, Tigger, Apollo, Pandora, Bingo, KaiKai, Jupiter, Pluto. The turnover was so fast there are many more I have forgotten. My dogs died of disease, of being hit by cars, of falling off balconies, generally of life expectancy in the Third World. Sometimes they were lost or stolen. When I was nine Apollo disappeared. For months I scanned the streets during every car journey. One day, a long way from home, on the other side of the city, I saw Apollo. The driver stopped the car. We opened the back door, pulled Apollo inside and drove off at speed. I never found out who had taken him or why; he had not been mistreated. Nor do I know whether we were seen as we effected his rescue. I imagine whatever witnesses there were remained silent for fear of being disbelieved.

The third child of my father and mother, and the youngest, I passed my earliest years as the beneficiary of what the experts call benign neglect. When I was three my father became active in politics. He was detained several times, once for three years. Amnesty named him a 'Prisoner of Conscience.' My stepmother kept the family together. I collected dogs. My parents, if they noticed, did not pass comment, even when the household total achieved a high score of six. I read *White Fang* and *Peter Pan* and longed for a wolf and a dog which slept at the foot of my bed. Ours were strictly yard dogs. Other animals passed through my life: a mongoose, a green parrot, a fawn. They interested me, fed my ambition to become a vet, but I did not love them. I loved only the dogs for reasons too complicated to elaborate upon, and yet also painfully obvious. In a time of lies, I found honesty and loyalty among the dogs. And if the memory of particular dogs has grown unreliable, then the memory of what they offered me in that time has become indelible: a retreat from the mutability of the human world, a place of safety.

There were a lot more vets back in those days. In the intervening years they have all gone—pursuing opportunities overseas, fleeing a civil war that lasted ten years and killed countless and uncounted numbers of us.

We arrive late. It is nine o'clock. Outside the school building people and dogs wait beneath a steady drizzle. The dogs are collarless, held on lengths of electric cable, nylon rope or string. A woman in pink holds on to a brown and white dog. A boy cradles a furious pup. A man arrives with a large black and white dog, which leaps and twists at the end of a long rope. Another man leads his dog on its hind legs, holding on to the front paws, like a dancing bear. Inside the schoolroom a line of people and dogs wait upon on a bench and impassively watch a technician gently shave the balls of a sedated dog.

This is a street clinic. Bring a dog here and you can have it sterilised for free. On other days Jalloh's team rounds up dogs from the streets, puts them in a wagon and takes them to the clinic to be vaccinated and neutered. The first time they tried to remove dogs local people chased them, demanding to know why the dogs were being taken and allowing them to leave only after the team promised the dogs' return.

'In Thailand,' Dr Jalloh told me from the wheel of his Land Cruiser on the drive across town, 'the authorities have a "keep your dog at home day." Everybody has to bring their dogs inside. Afterwards, they go through the streets and shoot any dog they see.' A few years ago the Freetown municipal authorities decided upon a similar cull of the street dogs. Dr Jalloh elected himself the dogs' representative and spoke during a public meeting. Though the odds were stacked against him, he argued that most of the dogs weren't stray but belonged to the community, that they—the dogs—performed a function and a service by offering security and protection. The mayoral dignitaries told Jalloh the dogs were dirty. Jalloh retorted that the opposite was true; their scavenging kept the streets clear of rotting rubbish. He had a point.

There had been no systemised rubbish collection in the city for decades. The authorities backed down; the dogs were reprieved. 'They say we are crazy . . .' he paused to answer his phone. The ring tone was a puppy's whine. They said he was crazy. And that was just the beginning.

In 1952, Konrad Lorenz published *King Solomon's Ring* in which he set out the terms of 'the Covenant'. The Covenant describes the relationship between human and canine, its beginnings and the stone upon which it is founded. A pack of jackals followed Stone Age man's hunting expeditions and surrounded his settlements, were tolerated, accepted and ultimately encouraged. Firstly for the warning note they sounded at the advance of predators, secondly for their ability to track game. The jackals, who initially followed the hunters in the hope of scraps and entrails, began to take the initiative, running before instead of behind the hunter, bringing to bay larger animals than they would be able to hunt without assistance. And so the Covenant was created, an interdependent exchange of services.

This is how, fifty years earlier, Rudyard Kipling described the origin of the Covenant in 'The Cat That Walked by Himself': 'When the Man waked up he said, "What is Wild Dog doing here?" And the Woman said, "His name is not Wild Dog any more, but the First Friend, because he will be our friend for always and always and always. Take him with you when you go hunting."'

For Lorenz, who went on to win a Nobel Prize, the contract between human and animal was 'signed . . . without obligation.' Jalloh, closer to Kipling than to Lorenz, would disagree. There is an obligation, it is unequivocal and one-sided. Having brought the jackal into his sphere, having bred the wildness from him, man owes dog.

Four, then five, then six freshly neutered and comatose dogs lie in a neat row, the paw of one lies across another, strange babies sharing a bed. An assistant tattoos the ear of each dog. There is a general air of understated chaos. Dogs roam the room. Outside a circle of children gather to watch as recently anaesthetised dogs stagger, circle and crash to the ground. The technician with the tattoo machine clips the ear of a reclining dog which, far from being sedated, is merely sleeping. The astounded animal jumps to its feet and stalks huffily away. Elsewhere, a technician attempts to inject a dog. It tries to bite him. The owner's efforts to hold on to his dog are so ineffective that the technician suggests the dog doesn't belong to him. The man insists otherwise. The waiting crowd wades in. 'He's afraid of you,' the woman in the pink top points out. A small boy steps forward and takes the animal. To me Jalloh says: 'Some people think they are the owners, but they are only the proxy owner. Usually the children are the true owners of the dog.' Sitting on the plane halfway across the Sahara two days before, I had suddenly remembered my rabies vaccination. I pulled out my yellow international health certificate, relieved to find there was a month left before it expired. 'Ah,' says Jalloh, cheerfully, 'but it is an inexact science.' He tries to keep himself inoculated, but the vaccine is rarely available in Sierra Leone. The staff wear doubled gloves. They have two or three muzzles in the surgery. That's the sum of it.

On our way back to the surgery we stop at the government veterinarian offices, which Jalloh is keen to show me. He jumps from the vehicle and leads me inside, introduces me to three men dressed in overalls and Wellington boots. The room is virtually empty of furniture and equipment. Dusty glass cabinets house ageing texts. The sole piece of equipment appears to be an old freezer. In one of the cabinets I find an elegant wooden box. 'Post-mortem kit,' says Jalloh. 'It will be empty.' I open it. Nothing, save the abandoned chrysalis of a moth.

As a child I'd owned a dog that overnight turned suddenly affectionate. Soon afterwards his hips locked. I carried him to the vet, walked him up and down to demonstrate the strange gait. The vet instructed me to bring him back if anything changed. The dog wandered and late one evening returned, his hind quarters split open to the bone by an axe wound. Through the night I tended him, feeding him raw egg with my fingers and following him around with a bowl of water, from which the wretched animal heaved itself away time and time again. I remember the episode now and recount it for

Jalloh. The dog was rabid. I worked it out for myself later. The vet had refused to admit it.

'"Craze dog" they call it,' says Jalloh. And tells an everyday story of his own. Some months ago, a woman brought three dogs to him for a regular checkup. In one Jalloh saw the tell-tale paralysis of the lower jaw. By the time the owner returned Jalloh had destroyed all three. He had no choice. It happens sometimes. In the slums the cry goes up at the sight of a drooling dog. Occasionally somebody will call him, but often by the time he gets there the dog is dead. Now that frustrates him, for diagnosis on a dead animal requires a post-mortem of the brain. If the dog were alive, he could gather a sample of blood. Jalloh likes to keep accurate records of such things. After all, nobody else does.

Gudush Jalloh was born in Kono, Yengema, in the Kamara Chiefdom. His parents were Fula Muslims, the nomadic cattle owners of West Africa who drive their herds through Mali, Senegal, Guinea and Nigeria. By the time Gudush was born in 1959, the first son of the first wife and eldest of twenty-two, the family had abandoned their pastoralist ways. Still, the knowledge of his heritage interested the young Jalloh. His early ambition was to own a herd. His mother reared chickens and the occasional goat; dogs played an early role in his life. When Gudush was fifteen his father arranged a marriage to a local girl, told his son it was time to leave school and join the family business as petty traders of gasoline. Gudush refused either to marry or to leave school, finished his education with the help of a scholarship and a former teacher who employed him as a part-time lab assistant. He began to apply for government scholarships to read engineering overseas. In 1978, he was one of a dozen who won scholarships to Hungary, but then, on the eve of travel, the scholarships were withdrawn and awarded to candidates with government connections. A year later he won a scholarship to Moscow. The African students arrived in Rostov in late September, without a word of Russian between them. They worried about how to make their stipends last, how to cook potatoes. Sometime during the year-long induction, Jalloh was persuaded by a colleague to switch courses and join him at the Moscow Veterinary Academy. He returned to Sierra Leone in the mid 1980s, the rift with his father healed by the prestige of having been chosen to study abroad. Jalloh tells me his father didn't mind that he had become a vet; he didn't know what a vet was. Later people said: 'So your son spent six years in Russia just to treat dogs?'

That year, the same year Jalloh returned, his younger brother, the second son of his father's third wife, was bitten by a dog. By the time Jalloh heard the news in Freetown, the boy had died of rabies.

Thursday. We are standing in the yard of an ocean-view house in the west of Freetown, close by the Mammy Yoko Hotel, where the great siege of the civil war played out. Guests hunkered down while the rebel troops of the RUF fought Nigerian-led ECOWAS troops and American helicopters said to hell with the no-fly zone, landed on the beach and evacuated their citizens and a few others as well. My stepmother was among those who had escaped. She told me how she was on the ship with a dozen working girls, scooped from the hotel bar and set down on the ship along with everyone else. They were excited. They thought they were going to America. Briefly, and for the first time, the world became aware of what was going on in our country.

From where I stand now, I can see terraced lawns reaching down to the waterside and an ornamental pagoda. No sign of the owners, a Sierra Leonean businesswoman and her European husband, or so I am told. There is just a watchman with a squint, a pronounced underbite and a diploma in passive aggression. The steward, who was supposed to fetch the prescription shampoo from the pharmacy and meet us back here, has still not shown. Teddy calls him. The guy swears he is on his way, but Teddy says he hears the sounds of a bar behind him. Dr Jalloh is not with us. He hates this kind of job, hates owners who don't know how to handle their own animals, who won't come to the clinic. Sometimes, he says, people just show him out to the yard, to a couple of half-wild beasts, and leave him there. He hates that more than anything. He's a vet, he says, not a dog whisperer.

Teddy, Zainab, Nabsieu and I are here to wash the dogs, but nothing is happening. We are standing in the eye of the sun while four dogs circle us, demonstrating various degrees of animosity. 'Here, in this situation, the relationship between owner and dog has reached total breakdown,' pronounces Teddy. 'These dogs no longer trust human beings. They will not allow themselves to be touched.' The dogs are flea-ridden and one has a skin infection. The exception is a tall, slim brown-and-white dog with a cropped tail. It looks healthier than the rest and allows itself to be petted. The dog came from next door. His Colombian owner turned out to have been the mastermind behind the planes local people would hear landing in the dead of night at the airport on the other side of the water. Motorboats from a small jetty in front of the house ferried the cargo to the mainland and from here the cocaine was loaded onto mules bound for Europe. Neighbouring Guinea has already turned into a cocaine state. After the Colombian's arrest the abandoned animal jumped the wall to join this pack. Teddy nicknames it 'the gangster.' One thing you can say about the Colombian though, he looked after his dog.

Twenty minutes on we get started. The watchman, who has been asked not to feed the dogs because we are about to administer an anaesthetic, is now giving one of them a plate of food. What is it with this guy? Poorly paid staff take out their resentment on the dogs, says Teddy. They sometimes feel the owners of the house care more for the animals than they do for them. Here the householders have been away for some months, which might explain the neglected state of the dogs and their hostility to humans. Ten minutes more are spent persuading the watchman to fetch soap and towels. Finally, we begin. Nabsieu inserts a dart into a hollow pipe, raises the mouthpiece to his lips and stalks the dogs with the quiet footfall of a hunter. The gangster goes down first. Nabsieu fells the remaining dogs one by one, a single dart each.

An hour later the job is finished. We have washed and scrubbed four dogs, searched for two in the nearby bush after the watchman opened the gate and let them out into the street. Now four dogs sleep it off in the shade. Zainab, Nabsieu and Teddy sign off on the job, telling the watchman they'll be back next month.

Back in the surgery Jalloh asks how it went. I say the whole thing is crazy. Jalloh shrugs and shakes his head. What to say? They service about twenty elite households in this way. The clinic needs the money. Maybe he'll dig a dip out back. Even so, he muses, people like that still wouldn't bring their dogs. He says that the main problem here is neglect. People don't have the money to care for and feed all these dogs, which I feel is broadly true, though the last two days have produced a strange, more complex picture. The slum dwellers' dogs are ten times healthier than the dogs of the country's most wealthy.

Lunch in a nearby restaurant and a conversation begun the day before is reprised. Jalloh has a television crew arriving from Holland in a week's time. On the drive back across town from the street clinic I'd asked whether he planned to allow the crew to film a clinic. Jalloh nodded. Some of what I had seen, I'd suggested, might prove unpalatable to Western viewers. A small silence. Jalloh wrinkled his nose and sighed: 'Oh dear,' and then, 'Europeans are so emotional.'

Ordinarily his tendency is to talk about the West in uncritical terms: as an animal nirvana where pets exist as legally protected family members. I wondered if this was a habit borne of the need to flatter, to treat everyone who visited from overseas—including me—as a potential donor. At the seminars and conferences Jalloh attends on his funded trips to Europe and America, the face the West wears is typically humane, rational, superior. Next to the representatives of international animal welfare programmes such as the RSPCA, whose reserves of £150 million represent twice our nation's annual revenue, Jalloh is the beggar at the banquet.

What the West reveals of itself at such times, naturally, is less interesting than what is concealed. In my street in London kids keep pit bulls, a dead pit bull in a bin liner turned up one day; dog fights flourish across the country. Now, sitting over steak sandwiches and Fanta, I detail none of this. Instead, I tell him about a photographer employed by a national newspaper magazine in Britain who was sent out to work with me on an assignment some years before. The woman suffered culture shock such that she was virtually catatonic, showing signs of recovery only within sight of the airport. Jalloh chuckles, his chuckle deepens into a laugh. Then for a moment he is quiet.

An American came to Sierra Leone to work for the Special Court responsible for trying war criminals, one of hundreds of lawyers and support staff employed by the American-backed court. She wanted to fly three street dogs to the United States and asked Jalloh to prepare the dogs for travel. He suggested she give the money to his programme instead. For the same money he could help a thousand dogs. She refused, spent $3,000 to transport the dogs. He remembers her name and repeats it. In time it will become a running gag between us, a byword for solipsistic sentimentality. It made him think he should be doing a 'sponsor a street dog' programme, like those for sponsoring children. Send a photograph of the dog and a monthly update.

That would work, I agree: 'She wanted to be a hero.' Jalloh repeats her name. Shakes his head and laughs.

Then there are those dogs, larger than the other street dogs, who roam the streets, tattered collars hanging around their necks. We call them the 'NGO dogs,' adopted by aid workers, abandoned when the contract is over. Not so very different to their relationship with the country. A departing staff member at the British High Commission recently left two dogs in Jalloh's compound before flying home for good. Last year the High Commission denied visas to two of his staff members who had been offered free training places at an animal centre in Britain.

And yet some people think it's Jalloh's enterprise that is misplaced in a country officially one of the poorest in the world. Then seventy-sixth out of seventy-six in the United Nations Human Development Index—a ranking we sometimes switch with Bangladesh. When last that happened, the president announced a national celebration. In the early days, Jalloh found himself turned away by the World Health Organisation and other international funding agencies, who told him animal welfare was not a priority. He argued, with incontrovertible logic, that human health and animal health were inseparable. He won.

The deputy foreign minister, lunching at a table nearby, comes over to say hello on his way out. The minister donated the old trailer Jalloh has converted into holding kennels behind his surgery, where a small shanty town is growing. Part of an old truck is being fashioned into a second unit. He keeps his vaccines in the freezer of the restaurant where we are lunching: the surgery is without electricity.

His is a makeshift existence. Before I arrived, Jalloh had emailed asking if I might help him obtain consumables for a VetTest, an elaborate piece of diagnostic equipment someone had given him. The cost would have come to €2,800; the materials required an unbroken cold chain between the factory in Holland and Freetown. The VetTest sits, unused, beneath his desk.

He tells me of a British woman who wanted to set up a dogs' home in Sierra Leone. 'Who would pay for it? Who would adopt all those dogs?' Of the international companies who offer him vast sums to exterminate the strays that roam their compounds.

The conversation will range over days: African pragmatism and reality, Western sentiment, the schism between the values of the two and the West's own conflicted treatment of animals. Jalloh's lot in trying to embrace, negotiate and reconcile so many ways of thinking. Here, a man presses a knife against a bull's neck, croons as he looks the animal in the eye and slits its throat. I have seen it happen many times and again recently. The occasion was a family celebration, the 'opening' of a house rebuilt after the war. A cow was to be slaughtered, cooked and fed to a hundred people. In the forest behind the house, five men prayed and held her until she died. The killing of an animal is attended with all the ritual of an offering. Indeed 'sacrifice' is the word we use.

In Britain factory-farmed animals, strung up by a single hind leg, inch along a conveyor belt to the screams of those who went before, emerging stripped of hair and skin, wrapped in cellophane.

I will ask Jalloh what he thinks of the dogs he sees in Europe, bred beyond the point of deformity for the show ring and the fashionable, a million miles from Lorenz's noble working dogs. Jalloh will smile and shake his head: 'And now they call our dogs mongrels.' I will repeat the conversation I had with my London vet, about the link between the physical abuse of animals and the physical abuse of children. Vets are under instruction to report every incident of animal mistreatment. Jalloh will listen, ask questions. Who are the perpetrators? What sector of society are they from? He frowns. No, he has never heard of dogfights here. In England he once trained as an RSPCA inspector, although he never went out on patrol. He read about the torture of animals. He found it 'interesting and very strange.' Another time he says: 'People here believe if you do something bad to an animal, something bad will happen to you.'

Once, I remember, I visited a hotel looking for a place to house a writers' conference the following year. A wild goose chase, as it soon became evident. The hotel had been abandoned since the war and was in an impossible state of neglect. In the bathrooms of a collapsed bungalow I found a litter of puppy corpses. The caretaker who accompanied me covered his mouth with his hand. 'Bad, very bad.' Nobody had seen the bitch for days; they'd searched for and failed to locate her pups. Perhaps she had been hit by a car. He shook his head, sure this was a portent of something terrible.

Says Elizabeth Costello, the protagonist in JM Coetzee's *The Lives of Animals*, in which the author uses a fictional setting to explore the moral argument about the treatment of animals: 'I do think it is appropriate that those who pioneered the industrialisation of animal lives and commodification of animal flesh should be at the forefront of trying to atone for it.' Trying to atone for a crime she compares to the Holocaust, a crime of 'stupefying proportions.' Costello's response is an ethical vegetarianism so extreme she is unable to sit at a table with meat eaters. On the other side of the table now, Jalloh has just completed work on his steak sandwich. I have never met a vegetarian in Sierra Leone. Perhaps because there isn't food enough to be fussy about protein sources. Or perhaps simply because there is a great deal less to atone for. In places where the distance travelled from Wild Dog and the creation of the Covenant is shorter, one finds neither the gas chambers nor the need to expiate, but rather a middle ground between the world of humans and the world of animals: a rough and ready equilibrium.

Still, it would be disingenuous to suggest crimes never occur. Jalloh chides me for my romanticism, reminds me, via email in our continued conversation some weeks later, that sometimes the knife is blunt. There is no singing. In Britain he finds people who care. In Sierra Leone they tell him he doesn't have enough work to do to be wasting time on animals.

The Sierra Leone 1960 Animal Cruelty Act, a parting gift from the departing colonials, sits unchanged upon the statute books. Jalloh wants it updated and enforced, he tells me. In the lifetime of the Act, there have been only two known attempts to bring a prosecution, both by Jalloh. Once against a man who beat Jalloh's dog. The man was a neighbour who had taken a dislike to the dog, a sentiment the animal heartily returned. The dog barked. The neighbour, when he thought nobody was watching, took a stick to it. Another time Jalloh attempted to prosecute a man who stoned a goat to death. The man claimed the animal had destroyed his crop; he'd warned it several times. Neither case reached the courts. The police treated both incidents as crimes of property. What struck me as I listened to Jalloh's telling, what strikes me still, was the history, the very personal enmity between victim and perpetrator at the heart of both crimes. There existed a relationship, a warped and angry one, but one that existed—something no law of property could ever take into account.

There were those who disapproved of Jalloh's actions, of the primacy he would give animals such that a man might be imprisoned. Jalloh would like to see rights for animals enshrined in law. Limited rights. The right to food and shelter. Not the right to life that animal activists in Britain would advocate. No, he shakes his head and thinks some more. Freedom from mistreatment, yes. An animal ombudsman, someone to enforce those rights. Someone like him.

Soon after his return from the Soviet Union, Jalloh collected fifty signatures on a petition, called a meeting and launched the Sierra Leone Animal Welfare Society. A young engineering student, Memuna, attended the first of those meetings. Two years later they married. An afternoon in the surgery they sit side by side and reel off the names of the other attendees by heart, produce the original minutes on translucent onion paper, offer them for my perusal, laugh and touch hands.

And then came war.

Jalloh and Memuna fled across land to Guinea. They carried nothing but his vet's bag and some antibiotics. Memuna was pregnant. 'I was worried she would abort,' he says. Abort, the terminology of a vet. In the Gambia they found sanctuary. Jalloh offered his services to the government, working on food security and cattle farming and, once, administering an NGO-funded programme to neuter the street cats that clustered in hundreds around the tourist hotels.

Two years later Jalloh and Memuna returned in time for the rebels' big push on Freetown. The street dogs grew fat feasting on corpses. People thought the dogs would go mad, Jalloh tells me, from eating the drug-addled flesh of the rebel soldiers. Though who could deny they did the city a favour? A doctor who worked at Connaught, the city's main hospital, described to me the days spent collecting corpses during pauses in the fighting. He found people's loved ones shoved down pit latrines, rebels left to the dogs. Once he tried to move the corpse of a young girl, a commander in the rebel forces, but furious locals refused to allow it. Leave her for the dogs. The fate she deserved.

The city was overrun with dogs. Jalloh chose that year to launch his campaign to protect them. More than once I have heard the story of how it all started. Now I hear it from his wife: 'He gathered eighty dogs and brought them to the compound,' says Memuna. 'I had to cook rice three times a day to feed them all. That night it was a full moon. The dogs began to howl. Next day I had to go to each of my neighbours to beg.' She laughs for a long time.

Today is Saturday. We are sitting together in the surgery, which she entered with wet hands, touching the back of hers to the back of mine. She excuses herself to return to the kitchen and oversee the cooking of tonight's feast. It is the first day of Ramadan.

It vexes Jalloh—the new fundamentalism spreading from Saudi Arabia, which has now reached even Sierra Leone. It breaks down the relationship between man and dog, he says. Teddy gives an account of a cleric who told one of his congregation to scrape the skin away from his arm where he had allowed a dog to touch it. At that Jalloh jumps up, begins searching for the papers upon which he has copied Hadiths about animals from the Koran. He talks fast and waves a finger in the air. He went on Radio Islam to talk about the treatment of animals under Islam. Now he's persuaded Alhaji Sillah, the city's chief Imam, to read out some of the Hadiths during Friday prayers at the Central Mosque.

In all the years of his life, Jalloh has never been diverted from his faith or his love of dogs. Only one thing came close to defeating him. His right eye, when it catches the light, contains a diamond-hard glint. I remembered hearing, when I was far away in England, that Jalloh was going blind. The glint is an intraocular transplant, an artificial lens. He is functionally blind in his left eye, having suffered severe optic-nerve damage and the resultant loss of ninety per cent of the sight. Two years ago he looked at the world through a tunnel of a six-inch span. He couldn't drive, could barely work although he carried on. The cause was cataracts.

On a trip to the United States, a friend, an animal lover and supporter of his, persuaded him to visit an optician. The eye doctor referred him straight to a specialist, who gave Jalloh six months before he lost his sight altogether. Jalloh had no money for the operation. The Dutch animal welfare agency who funded his work with the street dogs declined to help, informing him their funds were reserved for animals. Calls were made and the surgeon, who loved his two Labradors, agreed to waive his fees. Jalloh underwent the surgery but found he had overlooked the $10,000 hospital bill. The surgeon persuaded the hospital to cut the bill by half. Then came the $1,500 anaesthetist's fee. A phone call and he too waived his fee. So it went. This is how his sight was saved. For the love of dogs, says Jalloh, stands up and spreads his arms. But for the love of dogs, he'd be blind.

Saturday is the day the responsible middle classes bring their dogs to the clinic. Jalloh cleans out ear infections, administers antibiotics and vaccines—carried a half dozen at a time in an ice-packed Thermos from the restaurant down the road. At my behest he demonstrates the correct way to remove a tick: burst the body and let it detach naturally. Make the mistake of pulling and the head will remain inside. Dogs, his own, move freely in and out of the surgery. Jalloh, his assistants and I circle each other in the narrow space between his desk, examining table and shelves labelled: Orals/Endoparasites and Ectoparasites/Emergency Injectables/Injectables for Infectious Diseases, Catgut Suture Needles/Surgical Gloves. New supplies have been stuck in the port for two months now. His wish list for a far-off future: an orthopaedic surgical kit (most dogs are hurt in traffic accidents); a binocular microscope (he can't use his old

monocular scope because of his eyes); an auroscope and—
dreamtime now—solar power to run lights and a fridge.

We treat Emaka, Joffy, Fluffy, Cannis, Tiger, Rambo
and Combat. At two Joffy's owner comes to collect her dog.
Jalloh springs up and hands the woman a form for his latest
initiative—a license scheme, tells her to go to City Hall
and license her dog. Later he outlines the scheme for my
benefit. There is now a municipal bylaw, thanks to Jalloh
(one begins to believe the City Council has given up denying
him anything), which states every dog must be vaccinated
and licensed. The funds collected from citizens like Joffy's
owner are diverted to vaccinate and license the community
dogs. That's the plan anyway. The tax amounts to around
two pounds for a sterilised dog and three pounds for an
unsterilised dog.

Me: 'Is the law enforced?'

Jalloh: 'No. But it's enforceable. This is a test run. First,
we'll find out how much voluntary take up there is.'

Me: 'Has anyone actually licensed their dog yet?' There
being, in my view, no real possibility of enforcement in a state
still struggling towards a functioning police force.

Jalloh pauses, gives the habitual headshake, which I now
know signifies disbelief: 'No.'

And now I will tell you about the second time I met Gudush
Jalloh. It took place a few months after our first meeting, less
than two years after the end of the civil war.

I had taken into my home a street dog, a yellow-coated bitch.
I'd noticed her searching for scraps along the beach, checked
with some of the beach boys who confirmed that nobody took
care of her. With their help we bundled her into the back of my

car, where she stood on the parcel shelf and howled. The other
strays, who'd scattered at the moment of the kidnap, gathered
around the car, some howled back. A boy said: 'Dis 'oman dae
cam take you na heaven and you dae fom?' This woman has
come to take you to heaven and you're complaining?

I named her Mathilda and wooed her with corned-beef
sandwiches, just as I had on the beach. By five o'clock of our
first afternoon together she sat to my command. By six she
had learned to lie down. She became my companion during
the long days of writing. Several people asked if they might
have her when I left, for I had earned a reputation as someone
who knew a good dog. And Mathilda was a good dog; though
she never lost her skittishness around strangers, she gave me
her devotion entirely.

Then Mathilda was hit by a car. In the early morning a
man on his way to work passed a wounded dog lying in a
ditch, recognised her and brought her to my house. I drove her
to the only place there was, to Dr Jalloh's surgery. Mathilda
had two dislocated hind legs and, he suspected, a broken pelvis. He could try to slip the dislocated joints back into their
sockets, but not if the pelvis was indeed broken. With no X-ray
machine it was impossible to give an exact diagnosis.

The injured dog lay silent and still upon the table. A solution seemed unreachable. To attempt to relocate the bones into
a broken pelvis would be agonising and ineffective. I thought
I knew what Dr Jalloh was saying, I might have to put her
down. I stroked the top of her head. Then Dr Jalloh said he
knew one person with an X-ray machine. It was possible they
might let us use it. He offered to make the call.

Haja Binta, a Fula like Jalloh, had recently returned from
twenty years working for the NHS in Britain. Now she was

the proud owner of a small private clinic on the other side of the city. I arrived, carrying Mathilda who was partially sedated and wrapped in a towel. The people waiting to see the nurse thought I was holding a baby, but when they discovered it was a dog, they gathered around: 'Hush ya,' said an old man. 'Sorry-oh!' said someone else.

Haja Binta led us to the X-ray room and laid Mathilda on a steel bed, beneath the eye of the giant machine. Several times she repositioned the dog, pausing only to adjust her hijab. Afterwards she offered to develop the prints while I waited. I returned to the waiting room. After twenty minutes, Haja Binta came to find me. She smiled as she held up the X-rays. There was no fracture to the pelvis. The old man surveyed the images and gave a grunt of approval at the outcome. Somebody else said: 'Na God will am so.'

Mathilda recovered over time, retaining a distinctive sideways skip. One day, during dinner at the British High Commission, I told the story. My audience were mainly expats, people sent to the country in the wake of war for one reason or another. One man took exception to the waste of time and resources on an animal in a country where people had so little. He told me so as he walked away.

But, you see, here's why I think he was wrong. The people who had helped Mathilda: the man who reached into the ditch and brought her out, Dr Jalloh in his makeshift surgery, the Haja and her patients—they were Africans. They lived in the poorest country in the world. We were, all of us, two years out of a decade of civil war. We had survived the darkest place and we had all lost a great deal. This is Milan Kundera's test of humanity:

True human goodness can manifest itself, in all its purity and liberty, only in regard to those who have no power. The true moral test of humanity lies in those who are at its mercy: the animals.

I did not see foolishness or indulgence in all those people coming together on a single day to save the life of a street dog. What I saw was compassion, a sense of community, the sweetening of a soured spirit. In other words: I saw hope.

The Watch

For fifteen years I could not sleep. I would wake up in bed in our home in London at four o'clock in the morning, or three-thirty or four-thirty. Without looking at the clock I came to be able to estimate the hour with some degree of precision. In the winter months, when it was dark until at least seven, I'd lie for a while hoping I was wrong. In the spring I would play with the thought that the sky was merely overcast, clouds obscuring the dawn. None of these attempts to fool myself made any difference: for sleep, silvery, slip-skinned sleep, was already gone from my grasp.

Sleep left me in the year 2001. I realise now that my sleeplessness coincided with my decision to become a writer. My first book, the one I was working on then, was a memoir. It was tough—the excavation of facts and memories, the confrontation with both truth and lies. It consumed me. I began to wake up in the night thinking about what I knew, re-examining the past in the face of new facts, considering how I might discover what I still needed to know. I couldn't stop thinking. The next day I'd be edgy and aching but my mind never stopped.

When it seemed that my sleeplessness was not a passing phase, I began to practise what I discovered was called 'good sleep hygiene.' That is, I stopped drinking coffee after midday. I drank valerian tea before bed. Alcohol, nicotine, chocolate, TV—these are all stimulants. I stopped drinking wine after dinner. I did it, even though part of me is made sceptical by the way all good advice seems to start: by telling us to stop doing things we enjoy.

As the weeks wore on, I visited my doctor, who prescribed Zopiclone, a sleeping pill designed for the short-term treatment of insomnia. Sometimes the pill worked, or so it seemed, and sometimes it appeared to make no difference. The trouble was I didn't like the way I was left feeling the next day: as if the cells of my brain had drifted infinitesimally apart, whirring and whirring but not quite engaging.

For most insomniacs, getting to sleep is the hard part. This is called sleep onset insomnia. Peretz Lavie, an Israeli sleep scientist, studied the sleep patterns of civilians living in conflict zones during the Gulf War. During those nights people were too anxious about dropping bombs to sleep; once the bombs stopped they slept again. The causes of *sleeplessness* are varied and may result from external factors—noise and light pollution, caffeine, nicotine, alcohol, bombs dropping. Scientists don't consider this kind of sleeplessness to be the same as *insomnia*.

Lavie thought that (in the absence of any medical or external causes) sleep onset insomnia might become a learned behaviour. In an experiment at the University of California, researchers applied an electrical stimulus to a cat's hypothalamus: the area at the base of the brain which controls sleep. The cat instantly fell asleep. The researchers then sounded a note just before they delivered the shock. After a while the cat only had to hear the note played and it would nod off. Pavlov's cat.

So it is with humans. That is to say, for most people all the bedtime rituals are a preparation for sleep. Lavie noted that for the insomniac the reverse occurs: the bathing and brushing of teeth and hair, the settling onto a pillow, these only bring on a sense of dread. By the time they are in bed their blood pressure and heart rates have peaked. Caught in a loop, the insomniac's inability to sleep becomes chronic. To break the pattern, Lavie gives the opposite advice to the sleep hygiene disciples. Drop all of those careful routines and fall asleep fully clothed in front of a television.

I, however, self-diagnosed as suffering not from sleep onset insomnia (the condition Lavie describes) but from sleep maintenance insomnia. I could fall asleep; I just couldn't stay asleep.

The time before I can remember is when I slept best. As a child I slept in the back of cars, I slept on aeroplanes, I slept in a tangle of sheets, I slept in the arms of one parent while another remade the bed, I slept while they set me back down and turned out the light. On trips to my grandparents' house I slept in the big bed with my grandmother. I slept while she did not (she complained I kicked her in the night). As a child I slept. My own son, who is ten at the time of writing, sleeps. Thoughts of school don't keep him awake at night and nor do they cause him to wake with a start in the morning. What wakes him early on weekends are thoughts of play and the early-morning cartoons. He sleeps in during the week and, frustratingly for his parents, leaps up at dawn on the weekend.

A friend, who is also a psychologist, sent me a cartoon he thought I might appreciate. It went something like this:

Bladder wakes up in the night. 'I need the bathroom,' she hisses. 'Can't you wait?' asks Legs. 'I *really* need to go,' pleads Bladder. 'Do you hear that?' Legs says to Eyes. 'Okay,' replies Eyes. 'But nobody wake Brain.' So the sleeper heads to the loo, but somewhere on the way back Legs stumbles and bumps into a piece of furniture and with that wakes up Brain. 'What?' cries Brain. 'It's the middle of the night and we're up. I'm so excited! I just want to think about all the stuff we have to do today. Let's stare at the ceiling until they happen.'

'I think therefore I am,' says Descartes. What then does it mean to cease to think, rationally at least, for seven or eight hours each day? Do we cease to 'be'? Jean-Luc Nancy, another French philosopher, is of the opinion that when we sleep we become something else, another kind of 'be-ing.' In sleep we become another self, the dark self, in whom Nancy believes the soul and the mind are in harmony.

In his treatise *The Fall of Sleep*, Nancy contemplates the descriptive language of sleep, in which we are 'dead' to the world, the significance of the word 'fall' and the faith required of the act of falling. For Nancy, the insomniac is plagued by fear:

> He is afraid of letting go even of his troubles and his cares. He wears out his night in stirring them, in ruminating over them like thoughts bogged down in tautology, becoming viscous, creeping, insidious, and venomous. But what he fears above all else is not that the difficulties or dangers that these thoughts display threaten to arise as so many failures and defeats on the following day, what he really fears more than these fears themselves is leaving them far behind him and entering the night.

Psychological distress is the principal cause of insomnia, combined with a hair-trigger sympathetic nervous system, our so-called flight-or-fight mechanism. As I have said, I was writing a book that obliged me to revisit highly charged and sometimes dangerous episodes in my early years; also I have always been what you might call a 'light sleeper.' As these things go, I have a sensitive sympathetic nervous system. I'm the person who starts at sudden sounds and jumps if someone comes up unexpectedly behind me. In insomniacs the vigilance centres of the brain producing those impulses stay awake, while those of good sleepers close gently down.

Also, I am a lucid dreamer, which means that sometimes when I dream, I'm aware of the fact that I'm dreaming and can make conscious decisions within the dream. Only ten per cent of people are lucid dreamers. Once I dreamt I was about to skydive and that I felt afraid and unprepared. Then I thought, You know this is only a dream and you'll probably never get to do this in real life. And so I leapt through the open hatch of the plane. I have nightmares and will call to my husband to wake me up, and he often has. He says I'm not calling out but making muffled sounds of distress. Relief comes with the feel of his hand on my shoulder. Trying to escape a nightmare on my own is like being trapped in an underground tunnel. I have found no mention of an established link between insomnia and lucid dreaming, which itself was proved to exist by researchers only in 2013, but for me it stands to reason that someone whose brain is still partly awake might be both an insomniac and a lucid dreamer.

Most studies you might read put the figure of insomniacs in industrial and post-industrial countries at about a third of the population, and on the whole, these are not writers with a heightened response mechanism plus a history of childhood adversity. A third of people! After I discovered that figure I would keep coming back to it. Is there a tipping point at which a condition ceases to be considered abnormal? If half of us couldn't sleep seven straight hours, who would be the odd ones out? The ones who could or the ones who couldn't? When does a *dis*-order become the order?

My big problem was boredom: the tedium of being forced to pad around a cold, silent house where others were sleeping, trying not to step on an errant floorboard. There was no turning the sleepless hours into productive ones. I didn't feel like writing, at least not the book I was working on back then, but not any book really. It was frustrating. I wrote emails and found them to be filled with the exasperation I was then feeling, and so I stopped or I stopped sending them until I had reread them in a less strained mood.

I had then a dog, a black lurcher called Mab, after Queen Mab. Perhaps in naming her I already recognised the fickle relationship I had with sleep. I had once known Mercutio's monologue from Romeo and Juliet by heart:

> She is the fairies' midwife, and she comes
> In shape no bigger than an agate stone
> On the forefinger of an alderman,
> Drawn with a team of little atomies
> Over men's noses as they lie asleep.

Shakespeare's Mab bestows sweet dreams upon lovers and of curtsies upon courtiers, but when angered, Mab turns into a hag, whipping up nightmares and conjuring plagues of blisters upon the sleeping, frightening the horses and generally making things go bump in the night.

> Sometimes she driveth o'er a soldier's neck,
> And then dreams he of cutting foreign throats,
> Of breaches, ambuscadoes, Spanish blades,
> Of healths five fathom deep; and then anon
> Drums in his ear, at which he starts and wakes.

One night, I rose from my bed, urged my own Mab from her basket and drove through streets, in which not even the dustmen or sweeps moved, to Kensington Gardens. There were the others, among the outlines of the trees, the spectral figures of my fellow insomniacs. On different nights, driving through the silent streets, I became familiar with the solitary light in an otherwise dark row of terraced houses. The insomniac's beacon.

As a writer needs a room of her own, so does an insomniac. Once I couldn't sleep without my husband, then I couldn't sleep with him. During the worst of my insomnia he would go to sleep in the spare room. He is someone who can sleep anywhere and for however long he has. When we board a plane he is already poised for sleep, sometimes he doesn't even bother bringing a book on board, but tilts his head back and closes his eyes. As sleep grows more elusive, so the tools to entice it become more elaborate: the goose-down pillows, the sleeping pills, blackout curtains, ear plugs, eye masks. At some point I have tried them all, and at some point they have all failed me.

Gradually I grew to know the patterns of my insomnia. I'd wake up at four o'clock in the morning, usually following

a dream. I would start to ruminate. A writer always has
something on her mind. I'd lie awake and think about the
direction of my research, the line of my plot, the qualities of
my characters, whether I had fallen into the trap of cliché.
My brain would try out sentences, and then, if I arrived at a
pleasing phrase, knowing I would forget it in the morning,
I'd get up and write it down. I began to keep a notepad at my
bedside. Franz Kafka, Charles Dickens, Sylvia Plath, William
Wordsworth, the Brontë sisters, F Scott Fitzgerald and Walt
Whitman were all reportedly insomniacs. Some of those writers said insomnia was vital to their process, but I cannot say
that I ever felt it was vital to mine. It came to be part of it
though, and in time I knew there was little to do but accept it.

In those wakeful hours I would check the clock. I'd look
when I woke up, hoping I had managed to stay asleep until
seven or six. I'd even take five o'clock, for the difference
between five and four is that one belongs to morning and
the other to night. I'd check the clock every twenty minutes
thereafter to see how much time I had left before the alarm
sounded. Insomniacs, though, are not the only people in
the habit of counting up the number of hours we have slept.
Everyone does it. And everywhere I have ever been, people
will ask you how you have slept. How did you sleep? *Tu as
bien dormi?* Sleep has always been a source of concern. And
increasingly with reason, for today those of us who live in
post-industrial nations sleep on average seven hours a night,
nearly an hour less than thirty years ago and two hours less
than eighty years ago.

Reading Jean Verdon's *La Nuit au Moyen Age* brought
me to the discovery that the way we sleep now is not the
way we always slept. During the long nights of the Middle

Ages, sleeping habits were quite different and different again depending on whether you lived in the countryside or the city. For farmers, the working day ceased when the light went. Night began with the onset of darkness. Darkness meant danger, nowhere more so than the city. 'Fear of night, fear in the night,' writes Verdon. 'Fear of darkness amounts to a dread justified by nothing but the absence of visual perception. Man cannot live unharmed in darkness. He needs to see to act.' In European towns and cities night was announced with the sounding of the curfew bell. The city gates were closed, the drawbridge pulled up, people ceased work, went inside and bolted their doors until another bell announced the start of day.

Every house has a night-time ritual. In ours, in London at that time, we'd let the dog out and watch her disappear briefly into the darkness at the end of our long and narrow London garden. Before retiring we'd bolt the back door, top and bottom, turn the heavy iron key of the mortise lock, which for some reason had been fitted upside down by the Victorian locksmith, and finally, slide the barrel bolt. Every night the same performance was repeated at the front of house, and in winter we'd draw a heavy velvet curtain across the door against the draughts. Then we'd retreat upstairs and hunker down for the night.

Once we were robbed while we slept. The police told us there was a 'sneak thief' operating in the neighbourhood and we were not his first victims. He came in through the dog flap, which I had left open because by then Mab was ageing and infirm and needed use of the garden. I knew a human could fit through the flap, because I had done it myself when I taught her how to use the door. I explained all this to the police.

Also, how another policeman had once told me a story of how they had caught a burglar and, in his pocket, found a map. It showed an aerial shot of houses in the neighbourhood, some of which were marked with an X. When the police conducted visits, they discovered that those were the houses where the people owned a dog. The map was traded between thieves. 'This is pit bull territory,' I said to the policeman. 'Who would dare to stick their head into a dog flap that size?' But the police explained the thief had been watching our house. He knew that our dog was old and ill. He'd taken only a camera and a bit of cash, not much for the risk, you'd think. But for a sneak thief, it's all about the thrill. To get into your bedroom and watch you while you sleep. I'd had a bad cold and I'd taken a nighttime cold remedy to help me sleep. Simon had gone to the guest bedroom. Just that once, I wasn't awake.

Nights in the Middle Ages were long and so divided into what was called the First Sleep and the Second Sleep, with a period of wakefulness in between during which people might perform chores, care for children, bake bread or find a quiet place to make love—for communal sleeping was the norm and moments of privacy had to be sought out. In 1992, Thomas Wehr, an American psychiatrist, published the findings of a recent experiment in the *Journal of Sleep Research*. Wehr had persuaded eight student volunteers to spend twelve hours a night alone and in complete darkness. He found the volunteers soon settled into a pattern of sleeping for a total of nine hours out of the twelve, with a period of wakefulness in between. During the hours of wakefulness, they neither fretted nor fidgeted, but lay peacefully, in a semi-meditative state. In France this time was once called the *dorveille*, in England 'the watch.' Wehr's tests showed the volunteers had elevated levels of melatonin and prolactin, both of which promote calmness and contentment. During the day they reported feeling better rested and more awake, and by the standards of the sleepiness scale researchers used to check their wakefulness, they were indeed more alert. Writing about his findings, Wehr speculated whether 'the watch' had once long ago provided a 'channel of communication between dreams and waking life which has gradually been closed off as humans have compressed and consolidated their sleep.'

That makes sense to me. In Sierra Leone, among the Temne, we have a name for this place. We call it *Rothoron*, the liminal space between sleep and wakefulness. In the village of my ancestors, life hasn't changed that much over the centuries. People live by rice farming, and only the school building, where we have installed solar panels, has electric light. At night, on the verandah of each house, the yellow flame of an oil lamp burns. Otherwise the nights are so black, you cannot see your hand in front of your face. People retire early. *Rothoron* is the place (for it is considered a place and not a time) where the spirits and the living meet. In the morning the villagers greet each other much the way others around the world do, '*Ng dirai?* Literally, Have you slept? But meaning, Did you sleep well? Was the bed comfortable? I hope you were not woken by the cockerel's cry? The Temne mean all of that, and perhaps, Did you meet anyone in *Rothoron*?

In Croatia, in Smiljan, a village near Gospić, there is a memorial centre and a small museum marking the place where Nikola Tesla, the inventor of electricity, was born in 1856. In London, when I couldn't sleep and was out walking with Mab, I would sometimes go to the small park at the top of Telegraph Hill where we lived, which gave a view of the city skyline, the lights of which blanched the night sky above and irradiated the waters of the Thames below. It is strange but true that you don't have to go far beyond the boundaries of Gospić to find rural folk living much as they did during Tesla's time, without power to their homes and whose fresh water comes from a well. Nevertheless, it was Tesla's invention that dramatically changed the human relationship to sleep.

The first electrical systems were installed into factories and enabled production to continue after the hours of darkness. Workers were obliged to schedule their sleep more efficiently in order to meet those demands, such that now we sleep in a single, consistent block just once in twenty-four hours. We became what scientists term *monophasic* sleepers. In the late twentieth and twenty-first centuries emerged first, twenty-four-hour economies and soon, a twenty-four-hour *global* economy. This has meant that shift workers, that is, people who work in service industries, currency traders, computer tech workers who update office systems at times when they are not in use and the people who clean those same offices, truckers, flight attendants, medics, train drivers—all these people now don't get even seven straight hours but suffer irregular and disrupted sleep times.

As a result of these developments, research into sleep and the effects of sleep deprivation has increased exponentially in the last three decades. The first locus of interest was the military. Anthropologist Eyal Ben-Ari researched practices relating to sleep within the armies of industrialised nations and the way technology has been used to monitor the sleep of individual soldiers with the aim of maximising their fighting capabilities. In the mid-1990s, the US Army Medical Research and Development Command developed an elaborate 'Sleep

Management System' using information gathered in the Gulf
Wars. The system includes a wrist-worn 'Personnel Status
Monitor,' which records the amount of sleep a soldier has had,
combined with 'pharmacological agents to assist in the sleep/
wake cycle'—in layman's terms, 'uppers' and 'downers.' The
wrist-worn microprocessor is designed for efficiency—the data
is sent straight back to central command—and to bypass the
fallibility of self-reporting. It works by recording arm movements, in much the same way as my much later, mass-market
FitBit does. Central command analyses each soldier's data to
predict outcomes in performance for both individuals and
units. Soldiers are issued with two pills, one to induce sleep
and the other to return to a state of full alertness. Ben-Ari calls
these schemes ' "Cyborgs"—cybernetic mechanisms—those
hybrid machines and organisms that fuse the organic and
the technical.'

When I haven't slept for days, I wake faintly awash with
nausea. Life becomes like a bad dream, one of those in which
I try to run but my legs won't move. My thoughts congeal.
There seems to be a time delay on my responses. I know I will
achieve little that day, so I attend to paperwork and taxes. I
want to sleep but I can't. I become snappish. I wish everyone
would just shut up. As more nights pass, I reach for the chem-
ical cosh. I am fortunate in that my job does not require me,
except on certain occasions, to make split-second judgements
or to, say, hold a scalpel very still. In one of my novels, I wrote
about a surgeon whose insomnia was beginning to affect his
ability to do his job.

Lack of sleep causes lapses in attention, irritability, clum-
siness. After a while, affected people start acting like drunks.
When I first wrote about my insomnia, I talked to Martin

Moore-Ede who had acted as an expert witness for an airline pilot pulled over for drunk driving and ran a company called Circadian Technologies. He still does, only now CIRCADIAN 24/7 Workforce Solutions has offices in America, Europe, Asia and Australia and advises over half of the Fortune 500 companies. Moore-Ede first became interested in sleeplessness while working thirty-six-hour shifts as a trainee surgeon in the mid-eighties, left surgery to study physiology and later helped found a research laboratory for circadian physiology at Harvard. 'This is a hundred-year-old phenomenon,' he told me. 'We have basically created problems that did not exist back then.'

In the nineteenth century, for the rising middle classes, sleeping became a private rather than communal affair. Thus, today, we train children to sleep alone. We teach them to 'self soothe,' which is another way of saying 'cry it out,' with a blankie or teddy to replace the warm body of a parent or a sibling. Our schedules demand it and one day so will theirs.

Seis. Six. From the Latin *sexta*. Siesta. The arrival of darkness, the disappearance and reappearance of light, are only part of what determines a people's sleep patterns. Climate and geography play a role too. In countries where the temperature during the middle part of the day is too hot for manual work, people often retire to rest for an hour or so. These are the *biphasic* sleepers. Though the siesta is associated with the Southern European and Latin cultures, the tradition of a daytime rest exists across the globe. In China, Chairman Mao reportedly suffered from a twenty-eight-hour circadian rhythm as well as other sleep problems (according to Li Zhisui, Mao's biographer and personal physician from 1955 until Mao's death in 1976), which is widely believed to be the reason why the traditional midday nap was written into China's 1954 Constitution and has survived as Article 43 of the current 1982 Constitution of the People's Republic of China: 'Working people in the People's Republic of China have the right to rest.'

On June 1, 1944, in Mexico, the government, to widespread surprise, abolished the siesta for office workers. In the interests of the war effort, they said. According to contemporary reports in *Time* magazine and the *New York Times*, the journeying back and forth from home to office to home to office was putting too much strain on public transport, wearing out the buses. In addition, the long working day used up too much electricity. Before the change, the official office hours for government workers were ten o'clock until one o'clock and then four o'clock until nine at night. Imagine that.

In Spain, the siesta is said to be on the wane, as employers give in to the demands of a global marketplace, though in smaller towns it seems to hold still, for on my visits there I have always found it impossible to find a bank or a shop open at three in the afternoon. In the cities, even if people don't go home to sleep, lunch is taken at a leisurely pace at two in the afternoon, people work later and dinner is eaten at ten o'clock at night. An American I knew in Spain complained that during business dinners important matters were often not discussed until after midnight. The Spanish are holding out, at a cost, but they are holding out. The Chinese midday nap, for a period under threat from the same quarters, has apparently enjoyed a resurgence but for different reasons. Since the free-market reforms of 1979, China has become one of the world's largest economies. The long hours of production make it more profitable for employers to allow workers short naps at their desks, in order to sustain even longer hours.

The sight of a person whom I don't know sleeping bothers me. In the absence of the veil of the constructed self we wear when we are awake, it feels to me like seeing a stranger naked. Sleeping with somebody is an act of intimacy, even more than the sexual act, for lust is a very forgiving mistress. Sleeping together requires trust; each becomes the holder of the other's secrets: the nighttime cries or sleepy mutterings, the snores or farts. The public sleeper is at his or her most vulnerable, but doesn't seem to care. There they lie: slack-jawed, mouth agape.

And yet in many countries, people sleep in public all the time: the taxi driver in Morocco, awaiting a fare, tilts the driver seat back as far as it will go; the Indian rickshaw driver sprawls on the back seat, one arm flung across his eyes; the Brazilian office worker on a park bench. Sometimes anywhere will do. In Sierra Leone, I once sat opposite a slumbering legal clerk for twenty minutes, after which he raised his head, saw me there and said: 'How can I help you?' Looking back, perhaps it was his lunch break and he decided to have a nap. And why not? At the time I was outraged. In our world, time is money. And here was a man literally asleep on the job.

Not many women sleep in public though, and the reason for that doesn't require explanation. I, apparently, cannot even sleep in private. A boyfriend once told me he'd never seen me asleep. That whenever he rolled over in the morning, I'd be lying next to him with my eyes open.

Back when I first wrote about sleep, I said it was no coincidence that the polyphasic societies are often the poorest. Swiss sleep researcher Alexander Borbély observed the progression in humans from the polyphasic infant, through the napping or biphasic child to the monophasic adult. Sleep researchers saw this progression mirrored in societies as they moved from pre-industrial to industrialised. The thinking then was that the anarchic polyphasic sleeper would soon enough receive their wake-up call. But factories have been replaced by call centres, and the technological leap which has allowed some countries to skip the established route to industrialisation may in fact place them at an advantage in the future when it will be the people who are able to sleep anytime, anywhere—the flexible sleepers—who are most able to take advantage of the requirements of global networking. Today organisations from Google to NASA provide sleep pods and spaces with dim lights, eye masks and mood music so their employees can catch a pick-me-up power nap.

Sleep is a political issue. When and how we sleep is in the hands of authorities higher than ourselves. In Paris, in the eighteenth century, the masses demonstrated their anger against authority by smashing street lanterns. For them, artificial light was a symbol, not of civilisation but of oppression.

For a while I refused to give way to insomnia. I tried to accept my sleep patterns rather than fight it, resolving to work around it. Then halfway through a book tour, fractious with insomnia and jet lag, I telephoned my publisher from Chicago O'Hare Airport and begged to be allowed to go home. The next day I walked into the nearest pharmacy and bought an over-the-counter remedy, which you couldn't then buy in the UK, and which worked. I took the pills every night for the next nine years. Every time I went to the States, I bought new supplies and hoarded them. Then, four years ago I stopped taking them. I can't recall any specific turning point; I was just tired of it all. Also, I worried I might be addicted to the pills, which carried a warning on the label that I had chosen to ignore, much like everyone else I know who takes sleeping pills.

At first I suffered 'rebound insomnia' (what happens when you stop taking sleeping pills—the insomnia gets worse for a while). It is why so many people end up with dependency problems. I weathered it for weeks until my sleeping stabilised, or at least, until it fell into a pattern all of its own. These days I sleep about six hours a night. There will be periods—a week or so—when I don't sleep much at all, maybe five hours a night or less. Then I might tick up to seven hours for a while. Eight hours almost never happens. I find if I go to bed early, I will wake up in the early hours and maybe listen to an audio story or even finish the movie I fell asleep to a few hours before—'the watch.' One thing is true, the more I think about sleep, the less I sleep. During the nights between the days I spent researching and writing this essay, for example, sleep was scant. In contrast, during the 2020 coronavirus pandemic, and when so many others were struggling that newspapers carried articles giving advice to the suddenly sleepless, I started sleeping for eight or nine hours a night. Perhaps it was the monotonous rhythm of those days, of having nowhere to go or to be. I didn't find myself worrying, for the scale of the threat was so vast. Nothing to do but let go.

Now, in middle age, I find myself surrounded by newly insomniac friends, for ageing is a major cause of insomnia. Jet lag sharpens the desire to share stories. In Toronto, a woman told me about the cocktail of drugs she takes every night. 'One day you'll read about my death.' Another has started, in midlife, to smoke marijuana, now legal in that city and several states across America. In Vienna, a friend complained of the pressure of sharing a bed with her lover. Of reading by torchlight, like being twelve again.

In Cape Town, several time zones away from his home in Oakland, California, a writer I had just met asked how I had tackled my own insomnia. 'I tried to forget about it,' I told him. Maybe a year later he wrote to tell me he was doing a lot better. He figured that worrying about money was what kept him awake in the early hours. So he examined his track record and told himself that if he had been okay so far, he would be probably okay in the future: 'The skill of choosing to stop worrying about something,' he wrote, 'is proving to be versatile and extremely valuable.'

This can only be true.

Power Walking

Pretty Girl

I am twenty. I am walking along the King's Road in Chelsea, London. It is the 1980s. Three men are coming towards me; they are clearly together, though the foot traffic on the pavement requires each to walk a half pace behind the other. They are white, dressed in tight jeans and cap-sleeve T-shirts. The first man, as he passes, looks me in the eye and says: 'You're a pretty girl.' The second one smirks, but says nothing. The third one leans into my face and breathes: 'Nigger!'

My final year at university and I had a part-time job working for an American foreign correspondent. One of my tasks was to pick up the broadsheets each morning, and in those pre-Internet days I would leaf through them and clip and file any articles on the stories he was covering. That day was a Saturday in summer. I generally came in later on the weekend and the street was already busy with people. I was on my way to his house with my haul of newspapers when I passed the three men.

You're a pretty girl.

Nigger.

The first remark did not seem designed to offend. You're a pretty girl. It intruded on my thoughts, got my attention. Then came the complicity of the second man. Then, 'Nigger!' What happened afterwards? Do you imagine that the first man berated the third man? Do you think they argued? And whose side did the second man take? None of that happened. I know it didn't. You know it didn't. The three men carried on walking down the road. At some point one of them likely turned to the other.

And they laughed.

Walking

A child learns to walk. The child hauls herself up on a chair or her mother's knee, finds her balance and takes one tottering step and then another. The parents murmur sounds of encouragement, spread their arms. Come! Come! The father catches the child and swings her up in the air. My mother tells me that my approach was a little different from most infants'. I would crawl into the empty middle of the room and there I would take a breath and slowly rise. And I used my growing independence not to run towards her but to hasten gleefully away.

I grew up in the compounds of developing countries, in West Africa and Southern Africa, in the Middle East and East Asia. The hazards of the compound were snakes mainly, and army ants. As children, my brother, sister and I didn't leave the compound alone much except to go and buy sweets or when we broke out in search of adventure. Around the age of five I began to borrow my brother's clothes. Boys' clothes afforded a greater practical freedom, were better for sliding down bannisters, climbing trees, even the simple act of sitting. There was a lot of focus when I was growing up on making sure I sat properly, that is with my legs closed. My brother didn't have to sit that way, which seemed odd to me, given that he had something far more prominent to display. I wondered why, if what girls had between their legs needed to be so closely guarded, we were the ones to wear skirts.

I went to boarding school at six and left at eighteen for university in London. The enclosed worlds of compound life and British boarding school left me unprepared for the streets of the capital, the act of walking, specifically of walking alone as a female down a street. Yet in my tomboy/cross-dresser days, which lasted until I was around fourteen, I had already begun viscerally to understand something I couldn't articulate. I didn't want to be a boy; I wanted the freedom I saw belonged to boys but not girls.

2017. I am standing on the platform of a London Tube station back in the city where I lived for thirty years. A young man is looking at me. I ignore him, but his stare is intrusive. When we board the train he stands very close to me, and at one point his hand touches mine. I am twice as old as him, which makes this situation somewhat unusual. But everything else about it is familiar, and I'm old enough now to recognise exactly what is going on. The next stop is mine and so I move to stand facing the door. He follows and stands right behind me; I can feel his breath on the back of my neck. The train is crowded, it's unlikely anyone else has followed his behaviour closely enough to think it out of line. What the young man doesn't realise is that I am facing the wrong door. This is my old home station, and the doors behind us will be the ones to open. At the last moment I swing round and exit.

A week or so later, on the Tube again, I catch the eye of a
man sitting opposite me. For a few moments I hold his gaze
and then I look away. In the moment of turning I see him
smile and it is a smile of triumph. He has won something; he
has defeated me. Like the first man he is very young, around
twenty. In that moment I realise something chilling. My God,
I thought, he's *practising*.

Nobody tells young girls that men own the power of the
gaze. My mother never told me that men may look at me but
I may not look back. That if we do our look can be taken
as an invitation. Men teach us that. Over the years we train
our gaze to skim men's faces, resting for only a split second,
shifting fractionally sideways if our eyes happen to meet. The
man on the other hand, if he so wishes, will look at your face,
your breasts, your legs, your ass.

In her 1975 essay, 'Visual Pleasure and Narrative Cinema,'
Laura Mulvey describes how films are created to be seen from
the point of view of the heterosexual male. Their female characters are presented to him as objects of desire. This is the
'male gaze.' The gaze is power. Men own the power of the
gaze. White people do, too. A white friend tells me of the
time she took her adoptive daughter who is Black to a small
town in Maine and found her daughter the object of stares.
'I guess there aren't too many Black people in that part of the
country,' she suggests placatingly, because already I am visibly
irritated. 'And they don't own a fucking television?' I say. 'And
they've never laid eyes on their president or his family?' (This
was early 2016.) They stare because they can, by the gift of
the power vested in them by their membership in the ethnic
majority. They stare because her daughter's discomfiture is
nothing to them, it may be the whole purpose.

When a man stares at a woman in public her sensitivities are, at the very least, immaterial to him. He owns the power of the gaze and he will, if he cares to, exercise it. The real mindfuck is that enfolded into the action is its defence. The woman who complains may well find herself being told she should be flattered, that she is lucky men find her attractive.

'Where you going, baby?'

'Smile, little lady.'

'Sssssss!'

'Want some of this?'

'Look at the ass on that!'

'You wouldn't be able to walk if . . .'

''Til . . . it . . . bleeds.'

In the early nineties I shared an apartment in London's Chelsea. One week, while repairs to the roof were being undertaken, we had scaffolding erected at the front of the house. My room was on the top floor and faced the street, and from there I could see the roofers go up and down the ladders. At certain times throughout the day they would take their breaks sitting on the scaffold deck right in front of my desk unaware that I could hear them as they took turns yelling comments at the women passing in the street below. The excitement each opportunity provoked was astonishing. 'Here comes one, here comes one! Your turn!' One man in particular was actually jumping up and down on the scaffolding. The more evidently humiliated the woman, the greater the delight. From where I sat I noticed several things: firstly, yes, the young and attractive women drew more aggressive attention, as if the men were intent on denigrating what they could not possess, to punish the woman for being desirable and also unobtainable to them; secondly, no woman who was walking alone was exempt; and thirdly, they especially liked to pick on women who were dressed for work, who almost certainly earned more than they did. The women were metaphorically stripped, just as women were in earlier times and still are publicly stripped in some parts of the world, for transgressing the boundaries of womanhood, for stepping out of their place. They were being shamed, stripped not of their clothing, but of their dignity.

As a child I was taught to ignore aggressive dogs, to keep walking. Once you're out of its territory, the dog will leave you alone, so goes the conventional wisdom, and mostly it works. The same is supposed to be true of men, except it isn't. They walk alongside you; they kerb-crawl you. If you tell them to leave you alone, they will call you a bitch and ask you who the fuck you think you are. Every encounter, however seemingly benign, contains the possibility of violence. By the time it is over (you have entered a shop or a subway), your breath is coming quickly and your heart slamming against your ribcage. Why do men do this? Nobody asks the question and when I do, I don't get an answer. Sometimes it is said or suggested that this is simply the nature of men. What is interrogated more often is my response. Submissiveness is what is demanded. Women are taught not to answer back, for if we do we will escalate matters and then—the subtext—whatever follows will be our own fault.

Except I do, I do answer back. For, you see, it is in my nature.

In London in those early years, I get into fights. In South Kensington a man threatens to punch me after I tell him to piss off. I say I am going to fetch a policeman and if he is still there I will have him arrested. He swears at me, but he goes.

A man in Camden Town pulls out a knife and threatens to stab me in the stomach. A crowd, mostly white, gathers around me and watches to see what will happen. The man is Black and so am I. The standoff goes on for long seconds. 'Do you want to fuck with me? Do you want to fuck with me?' Even then the ghost of a joke crosses my mind. Well, I thought I'd made it perfectly clear. Another man, also Black and wearing dreads, moves through the audience. He walks up to us both, looks at the man with the knife and says: 'What's the problem, brother?' I never see that man again, not even to thank him, because the friend with whom I am walking has found a policeman and my harasser flees. But he is caught, and he goes to court and I am there, and I see him. His hair is braided, and he wears a shirt and suit; he looks so different I wonder if I would have picked him out of a line-up. My statement is read to the court. He is found guilty, not of the sexual harassment which began the whole altercation, although the judge tuts at this part of my statement, but of possession of an offensive weapon. The case is over in minutes, my assailant is sent away to be sentenced at a later date. The girl I was walking with and her father attend the case. They both make it clear, though not unkindly because I have now learned my lesson, that this is my fault. Later, when I tell the story, I will discover that in the eyes of many of my white friends, the fact that I am Black and both my harasser and saviour are Black, makes this a 'Black thing.' Something in which they have no stake and in which the mostly white onlookers are now exempt from interfering; the courage of the dreadlocked man is suddenly not so great.

On the streets race and gender intersect, the dominance of men over women, of white over Black, of white men over white women, of Black men over Black women, of Hispanic men over Hispanic women and so forth. Layered upon that is the relationship between men, the sometime competition and sometime complicity between men of all colours, the upholding of male power. This can play out in a variety of ways. For a woman of colour, men of the same ethnicity may be ally or foe.

In London men view street harassment as an equal opportunities' occupation. I've endured sexually aggressive behaviour from men of every colour and class. In New York I am rarely *publicly* bothered by white men. How to account for the difference? In America the edges of racial politics are sharper and more bloodied. Human motivations are often hard to fathom, but I'd give a good guess that white men in New York City are scared to be seen harassing a woman of colour. To be *seen* to. In *public*. There is also this—that within the codes of heterosexual masculinity, Black men have ownership of and therefore power over Black women. In some places this code is more strictly enforced than others. On one of my last visits to the city I had to pass a group of workmen on a narrow pavement as they stood leaning with their backs against a building. In London this would be an inescapable moment. But we were in New York. All the men were white except one Black man at the end. I was dragging an overnight bag and so progress was slow. The men went silent and watched me as I passed. The unspoken rule, I sensed, was that the job of calling out to me belonged to the last man, the Black man. I walked towards him and it seemed we both knew what the other was thinking. Would he betray his race or his place in the patriarchy? As I passed, he leaned forward and, audible only to me, whispered: 'I like your jacket.'

Emmett Till was murdered. Emmett Till did not own the power of the gaze, at least not as far as Carolyn Bryant was concerned. Fifty-plus years on, white women friends in New York complain of the behaviour of some Black guys there. They worry about being thought racist if they complain. This is the power play between men, the revenge exacted by certain Black men upon white women but, in reality, upon white men. Payback is the pickup truck bearing a Confederate flag that cruises me twice on a long, lonely run in Western Massachusetts, the white guy with the baseball cap who turns his head and licks his lips on each pass.

#NotAllMen

At some point most women come to the silent and terrible realisation that the men in their lives—fathers, brothers, uncles, boyfriends and husbands—are not especially outraged by their experience of sexual harassment.

Late one evening when I was in my mid-twenties I had a row with my then boyfriend. I decided to go home until I remembered the time of night, that I didn't have a car and would have to call a taxi if I hoped to execute my walkout. I had very little money at the time and I'd have to weigh the cost of the taxi against the level of my outrage. A few months later, arguing with the same boyfriend (things didn't last too much longer), while on holiday in southern France, I remained walking on one side of the road while he crossed to the other. We were headed for the beach and the road was more or less empty. A man driving by, assuming I was alone, began to proposition me. I ignored him for a few moments and then I told him to get lost; finally I crossed to walk with my boyfriend and the man drove away. I remember very well my boyfriend's reaction—he laughed at me.

Writing about South Africa, where the incidence of rape is among the highest in the world, the feminist activist, poet and academic Helen Moffett has stated:

> Under apartheid, the dominant group used methods of regulating blacks and reminding them of their subordinate status that permeated not just public and political spaces, but also private and domestic spaces. Today it is gender rankings that are maintained and women that are regulated. This is largely done through sexual violence, in a national project in which it is quite possible that many men are buying into the notion that in enacting intimate violence on women, they are performing a necessary work of social stabilisation.

In other words, rapists are the shock troops of male power.

The more I think about it, the more I come to the uneasy conclusion that, whilst #NotAllMen are rapists or sexual harassers, equally #NotAllMen are too unhappy about the status quo either. The relative vulnerability of women in public spaces limits our freedom of movement and our choices. Good practise in personal safety—telling someone where we are going, allowing ourselves to be escorted home and not walking alone at night—all add up to an effective form of social control. 'The necessary work of social stabilisation.'

Only in the second half of the twentieth century did middle-class women in many Western countries acquire some degree of freedom outside the home, and before that to walk unaccompanied was to be taken as a prostitute, a 'woman of the streets,' a 'streetwalker.' Walking, for a woman, can be an act of transgression against male authority. When a man walks aimlessly and for pleasure, he is called a flâneur, a certain louche glamour attaches to the word. One rarely hears the term flâneuse. In her account of women walkers, itself called *Flâneuse*, Lauren Elkin observes: 'Narratives of walking repeatedly leave out a woman's experience.' Historically, the free-ranging woman who dispensed with the domestic to claim ownership of the streets was a rare creature. Virginia Woolf, Jean Rhys, George Sand, the flâneuses who recorded their flânerie were women who all defied male authority in other ways too. George Sand wore male dress so that she could move more freely around Paris.

Only once has a man ever stood up for me against harassment by another man (with the exception of the guy with dreadlocks, though he did not know what had started the trouble) and the man who did so was gay. We were standing outside a bar in Soho in London, smoking cigarettes, when a young man passed me and made a remark to which I responded with a put-down. His rage was instantaneous. He was smoking too and he threatened to burn me with his cigarette, holding the lit end close to my cheek. My companion intervened and in doing so drew fire away from me, literally because now the burning cigarette tip was being held to his neck. The scene ended when a friend of the assailant's pulled him away. Afterwards we talked about it. I observed that a straight man would almost certainly have reprimanded me for my comment but he, notably, had not. No, he told me, because he grew up having much the same fight on the streets: the sexual insults, the shouted provocations. As a gay man he had learned to stand up to bullies.

Yet when I have talked to straight men about what happens to me on the streets, I have consistently been met with looks of blank innocence. They insist they know nothing of it. I have seen the same conversation played out extensively on social media where the men most devoted to the use of the hashtag #NotAllMen always claim ignorance, are 'surprised,' so 'surprised' they'll go as far as to deny that what women are telling them can possibly be true, that invention or exaggeration on a global scale must surely be in play. Talking to a straight man about street harassment can be, as many Black folk including Black men have pointed out, like talking to some white people about the daily indignities of racism.

Somehow, something enacted in broad daylight thousands of times across the life of virtually every woman has gone entirely unnoticed by most straight men. At some point you have to ask: How can it be so?

How can it be so?

On Matriarchy

I am driving down the road from my home in Freetown when a youth makes a kissing noise at me. I brake hard, bringing the car to a halt. 'Did you hear that?' I ask the friend I have with me. She says she did. 'I don't believe it,' I tell her. To the young man I say: 'Come here!'

I expect this kind of behaviour in many places, but I have not experienced it in the city where I spent many of my formative years. The youth, in his late teens or early twenties, is leaning against a wall in the company of four or so friends. One of them nudges him and points to me. He pushes off the wall and approaches the car; he saunters over but his cockiness has already lost its edge. People are watching, not just his mates but the women stallholders on the other side of the road and a couple of passers-by, too, have stopped.

As I have said, I grew up in several countries in the world, and as an adult I have travelled much of it. In every city and country I have ever visited I make tactical decisions before I step out of the door. Time of day, clothing, route: these things must be considered. Often this is done at a subconscious level; other times advice might be sought or given. There is a constant tension between the desire to look one's best, to be noticed, and the price that will exact. I want to dress for my destination, the person or people I am going to meet or the event I am headed for, but I must also dress for the men I do not know who I will encounter along the way. Anonymity is something I can only imagine, to walk unguarded an impossibility. Certain places, though, are better or worse than others.

When I start in on the young man in Freetown, he apologises almost at once. 'My name is Aminatta,' I tell him. 'And the next time you see me you will remember that and you will use it when you greet me.'

'Yes.'

'Yes what?'

'Yes, Aminatta.'

'No!'

The youth looks startled.

'Yes, *Aunty* Aminatta.'

'Yes, Aunty Aminatta.'

Sierra Leone is what some anthropologists have called a 'matriarchy posing as a patriarchy.' It is also a gerontocracy, and deference is expected of anyone younger towards anyone older, even if only by a few years. Over lunch I tell my stepmother what has happened and she laughs. 'Oh, it's those little dresses you wear. They think you're younger than you are.' My mother, sitting sideways on her chair like a Victorian lady riding side-saddle, is wearing robes arranged in swathes around her. I am wearing a cotton shift dress and sandals. Then: 'Anyway the NGOs brought all that here with them,' she waves a hand as she sips her ginger beer. Freetown then was home to hundreds of Western aid workers, newly arrived in the wake of war. There's a tendency to blame unpalatable social behaviour on outsiders—and yes, everything about those young men (the sagging jeans, the backwards-turned baseball caps, the sullen expressions) spoke of an enthusiasm for American rap—but my stepmother is saying something different. She is saying, they were treating me as if I were a Western woman.

On my first visit to Ghana a couple of years later, I have a series of similar encounters: in a hotel a young man in baseball clothes murmurs suggestively as I pass by. I stop and I yell at him. His companion, an older man in a business suit, turns and looks at the young man open-mouthed and orders him to apologise. As they walk away, he continues to gesture angrily. The porter with my suitcase asks me what the young man said. He shakes his head: 'They send them to America, you see.' A few days earlier I had taken a walk down the beach at another hotel. There were men working on the scaffolding of a building, and one of them called out to me. I stopped and shouted at him: 'Is that how you talk to your mother?' A local friend who I tell later on will smile at this point in my story. 'So they realised you are an African.' On my way back I had to pass the men again, and I was a little concerned about how the next encounter might go, but the men were silent.

I won't make a host of claims about the position of women in West African society, nor will I say that a man will never speak or behave insultingly to a woman in a public space. But

I will say this, if he does and if she makes it her business to reply, she can expect the crowd to have her back.

Whose Space? Loos, Queues and Other Places

When I was still at college, I read in a newspaper of a study purporting to show that when a man and a woman are walking towards each other on the pavement, the woman invariably steps aside for the man. I told my flatmate about it, and the next time we went out she announced gleefully: 'You're doing it! You're doing it!' Ever since then, whenever I think about it, I try to hold my ground and have often found myself nose-to-nose with men who are evidently so used to the path clearing ahead of them they can't figure out where I have come from. In the last year or so the discussion has resurfaced and now the behaviour being described has its own portmanteau: 'manslamming.'

In July of 2017, *New York Times* reporter Greg Howard, a Black man, accused white women of doing the exact same, writing: 'When white women are in my path, they almost always continue straight, forcing me to one side without changing their course. This happens several times a day; and a couple of times a week, white women force me off the sidewalk completely.'

Earlier in the same year I was standing in line for the ladies' in a theatre in Baltimore. The theatre was under renovation, some of the facilities were closed and the line was about fifty-people long. Women were making way for very old women and women with disabilities, allowing them to jump the queue. The crowd that night was mostly white, and by chance I found myself standing next to the only other woman of colour in the line. A white woman, older (but not so old she might have skipped the queue) and evidently wealthy, walked down the line, stopped halfway and inserted herself just in front of me. I looked at her. I looked around. I caught the eye of the African American woman next to me. 'Did that just happen?' I asked. She raised her eyebrows: 'Don't say anything,' she mouthed. But I did. I said: 'Do you just do that then? Stand wherever in the line you want?' and eventually the white woman slipped out of the line and walked to the back. I asked the African American woman: 'Was it just a coincidence that she stood in front of *us*?' And she replied: 'I'm saying nothing,' and gave me a look like I had been born yesterday.

I return to Helen Moffett who pointed to how, during apartheid in South Africa, the dominant group, whites, had used methods to regulate blacks in public spaces in ways which reminded them of their subordinate status. It's all about power, people endeavouring, consciously and subconsciously and through myriad daily encounters to establish dominance over those they consider less worthy. During the Jim Crow era in the US, white Americans forced upon African Americans the same ignominies as white South Africans did upon their black populations, reserving certain public spaces and privileges for whites. When Black people challenged this orthodoxy, it's no coincidence they did it, just as black South Africans did, by walking, by marching, by crossing into those spaces barred to them.

Greg Howard asked an Asian friend, a man, whether he was forced off the pavement by white women on the streets of New York. The answer was no. It was the white men who ploughed through him.

Three years ago at a friend's book launch I was standing talking to a man I always liked to talk to whenever we met. He was (he has died since) tall, six foot two or three, and still broad-shouldered though he was then in his eighties. We were standing close to the bar, and I was telling a story and turned at one point to find his face suffused with rage. I wondered what could possibly have happened, and I asked him if he was all right. 'He would never, ever have done that thirty years ago,' he eventually said in a low voice. A man on his way to the bar had shouldered him. 'As if I wasn't there.' He'd been manslammed.

I am as certain as I can possibly be that this man had never catcalled a woman, probably was even the kind of person who stepped aside for other people on the pavement. By the same token, I am equally certain he has never endured a carload of women hurling obscenities at him, heard a woman hiss filth into his ear as he waited to cross a road, or seen a woman waggle her tongue and clutch at her crotch. I remember his face, the mix of fury and frustration, how taken aback I was that he could be so angry, because worse happened to me on any given day.

As I write this, I wonder about all those guys, of every class and colour, who have interrupted my thoughts in order to remind me of my place. For whom it was fun to try to unnerve or to humiliate me. To them I say, just wait. It's coming. Too late for me. Too late for you to learn much except a mote of what it might be like to be treated as if you don't matter. But it's coming.

I'd like to say I wish I were a better person than to feel that way. I wish I could. But I can't.

What If You Gave an Inauguration and Nobody Came?

'We'll need to get out at Adams Morgan and walk. We'll never make it onto the Mall, in any case.'

Two of us are on our way to the inauguration of the 45th. Up until a day or two ago my plan had been to attend the event alone. I didn't know too many people who might want to come and my husband knew well enough the calculation I had made when I told him I was going and suggested he stay home with our son. It was likely the event would attract white nationalists and we both knew the sight of a racially mixed couple inflames folk such as those like little else. Alone, I made a far less enjoyable target. This sounds counter-intuitive to some people. It certainly sounded so to a colleague at the university who offered to come along. 'You need someone with you.' I said thanks but no, finally I explained carefully that I didn't want a white man with me. 'But I'm not "white,"' said Duncan, which was technically true. Duncan Wu's mother is white British and his father is Chinese, but you couldn't tell this by looking at Duncan. On matters of my own safety, I really prefer to trust my own judgment. Still, you know how it gets.

'We'll need to decide a place to meet if we get separated,' says Duncan as we ride the subway escalator at Adams Morgan station. I'll admit that letting Duncan accompany me is turning out to be not such a bad idea, because Duncan had been at the inauguration of the 44th, and knew a thing or two. All the same and for aforementioned reasons, I'm not overly concerned about becoming separated from him. I say: 'How about we meet back home?' But Duncan insists he must not leave me alone, so I suggest we regroup at the Metro station. Duncan describes for me the last inauguration: cold that numbed cheeks, hands and lips, crowds so dense movement was at times impossible and at others impossible to resist, jammed cell phone networks—the reasons we need to agree on our rendezvous now. We step off the elevator and out into the street. It is empty. A lone jogger passes us by. Duncan frowns and looks around. I'm still not used to the geography of DC, or sure of exactly where we are. I think we must have got off at the wrong stop and suggest we get back on the Metro. But we haven't and we don't. Instead: 'We'll walk,' says Duncan.

And so we do. We walk past merchandise vendors, we walk past Secret Service men and women, past police horses in their boxes, we walk past barricades. Everything you'd expect at an inauguration is there, everything except for people. Duncan and I take photographs of each other, one against the backdrop of the Lincoln Memorial. I take a picture of a row of unused lavatories, of Black street vendors selling red baseball caps. Duncan is British and by pretending to be a visitor he takes to gently baiting Secret Service officers. 'Is something going on today? Is something supposed to be happening?'

At Constitution Avenue, by the memorial to the Vietnam Veterans, we find people gathered in a cordoned-off area of the park. There is an enclosure and inside the enclosure something approaching a crowd. A small group of protesters wave signs outside. A white couple pass by (pretty much everyone apart from the vendors is white). The woman has on a camel coat and her hair is the kind of luminous ash-blonde I equate with the very wealthy. She turns to one of the protesters—middle-aged, pudgy, he looked like he might teach high school—and with a toss of her head says: 'We won!'

I've come looking for supporters and here are some. We join the queue for security, but soon realise that all gaining entry buys us is a view of a giant screen and limited escape routes, and so we slip out of line and head for Independence Avenue. There we find three men holding up signs which read: 'I'm a Muslim' and 'Meet a Muslim.' But nobody is taking up their offer, mainly because there is hardly a soul there. There is one couple who look like foreign tourists, real ones this time, who had maybe thought it would be nice to be in DC to see a presidential inauguration (this idea having arisen many months ago when they booked their stay) but haven't quite banked on this, a city that feels like the start of one of those films—you know the kind—when the hero wakes from his hospital bed and wanders through deserted streets still in his patient gown.

From Independence we walk to 12th Street, where we find a security check. No lines this time, and so we sweep through. A banana among Duncan's possessions is confiscated. Maybe they think he plans to throw it, I don't know. It starts to rain. Now we can see on the screens at each intersection on Pennsylvania Avenue that the swearing-in ceremony is under-way. Small clusters of people in a few of the bleachers, which are otherwise empty. We are only a short walk from Trump Hotel and we agree surely there will be crowds there, but we are stopped from reaching the hotel by the barriers that have been erected to partition off sections of Pennsylvania Avenue, a crowd-control tactic which in the current situa-tion has become utterly redundant. Still, we can see all we need, namely that the pavement outside the hotel is empty. We watch the president-elect take the oath, debate whether to wait for the motorcade and decide not to. I imagine the 45th driving down the near-empty streets, on a day like Miss Havisham's wedding day.

The 45th will take it with none of Miss Havisham's for-bearance. His spokesman will say the turnout was the largest of any inauguration. Others among his followers will accuse the park service of doctoring the photographs of the Mall which show how much greater had been the turnout for the 44th. The 45th will insist that the sun shone.

On a deserted Memorial Bridge, Duncan takes a selfie and I take a photograph of Duncan taking a selfie. Outside the gates of Arlington Cemetery, where I have arranged for my husband to meet us and drive us home, we see our first and only white nationalist. He wears a sharp haircut, white shirt, black jacket and long britches tucked into jackboots. He is walking in the opposite direction from us, and I know not where he has been or where he is going.

At home I upload my images onto Facebook, first of all one that Duncan took of me sitting alone in the empty bleachers, and underneath it I type: 'What if you gave an inauguration and nobody came?'

Bruno

We stood with our backs pressed to the outside wall of a wooden shack. A few yards away rose the wire fences of the enclosure. We were three: my husband, the keeper and me. The keeper turned and said: 'Madam, when I say run, you run.' He pointed to another shack about twenty yards distant. He had a lazy eye, which was all I really had time to notice before he said: 'Run, madam! Run!' I set off. About ten yards in, a rock came hurtling over the fence and hit the ground a few feet behind me. I ran faster until I reached the other hut, where I stood and watched my husband dodge a second missile. After that came the keeper, hopping across the uneven ground in plastic sandals.

'What was that?' I said.

'That was Bruno,' the keeper said. 'He doesn't like people and so he throws rocks.'

I looked around the corner of the hut. There was an ape, huge and upright, holding a small boulder above his head. In front of him stood a pile of rocks, stacked like cannonballs.

'And you sent me *first*?'

'Madam,' said the keeper, whose crooked gaze somehow lent him a look of candour. 'His aim gets better.'

My son, then eight, laughs, a great belly laugh, uncommon in a child, even though he has heard the story several times. The scene I'd just described had taken place ten years before he was born. At this age, our son likes to hear true stories, in particular those from my childhood, of adventures in overseas lands, of how I met his father, tales of my years in boarding school in England and of corporal punishment, the idea of which appals and thrills him. I think perhaps he enjoys these stories for the same reason I remember liking those of my parents' stories from the time 'before me,' which was to my mind some unimaginable dimension. This is my third or fourth recounting of the story of Bruno, the ape.

Bruno is a legend in Sierra Leone. In 2000 I had returned with my husband for the first time in nearly a decade, during which a civil war had raged, the last embers of which now burned across a cindered landscape. People needed help, money, solace, and we tried our best to give them those things, visiting and receiving several times a day, listening to stories of loss, giving where we could and helping plan for a future few people had even dared dream. One day, in need of an afternoon to ourselves, we went to the ape sanctuary a few miles outside Freetown to relax by pretending to be tourists. Tacugama Chimpanzee Sanctuary had been started by a Sri Lankan expat some years before, and he was there when we arrived, sitting cross-legged inside one of the cages, holding a baby bottle to the lips of an infant chimp. Visitors were rare, and we waited while he found and seconded a keeper to act as our escort. Soon after came our game of dodgeball with the alpha, Bruno.

In 1988, passing through a village in the provinces, Bala Amarasekaran and his wife, Sharmilla, came across an orphaned baby chimpanzee whose mother had been killed in a hunt. For twenty dollars they took the chimp home and named him Bruno, after the British heavyweight boxer whose title fight against Mike Tyson was due to take place the same day. Within a few years the baby had grown into a juvenile, already as strong as a man; a full-grown male chimp has easily one and a half times the arm strength of a human adult male. Smart, affectionate and inquisitive, Bruno was also destructive, possessive and territorial. One day Bruno attacked a workman who had come to the house. It wasn't the first problem the pair had had with him, but it was the one that made them decide they couldn't keep him at home any longer. By then they'd already adopted, as company to Bruno, a second chimp, a female called Julie who'd been abandoned by a departing expat. The idea for a chimp sanctuary followed, and there was no shortage of animals, adolescents typically, some given up reluctantly by owners who'd lost control of their former pets, others rescues who'd arrived injured or scarred.

I've only ever known one chimp. His name was Cuba. I met him at the house of a friend of a friend when I was in my twenties. He didn't like people much and he disliked men in particular, though he loved the steward who took care of him and, I was told, he had been known to take a shine to a woman visitor or two. One day, walking alongside me, Cuba reached up and offered me his hand. Pleased at this sign of friendship, I took it. I thought, Cuba likes me. Cuba's hand was huge, long-fingered, dry, and he held on to mine with a firm grip, one that grew in pressure until I felt my knuckles grind against each other. I told him to stop. He didn't. I stood still and turned toward him. Stop it, I said in the voice I use for disobedient dogs. Cuba stared at me unflinchingly and tightened his grip. I cried out. The silent-footed steward appeared and hissed Cuba's name. Instantly, Cuba released me and bounded over to the man, who turned and walked away, the ape at his heel.

Chimps should never be pets. When I look back at Cuba, I see how disturbed was his behaviour. He spent hours of his day chained to a pole frame from which he swung, one hand on the bar, the other gripping the chain around his neck that otherwise threatened to strangle him. A lot of young Lebanese men were visitors to the house. Cuba's party trick was to smoke cigarettes. He would ask a visitor for one, pointing at the open packet, and then he would perform, placing the cigarette in his mouth to be lit and gambol off to swing on his frame, holding the cigarette between two fingers and puffing on it to the sound of laughter. I remember, too, that he masturbated a great deal. Excessive self-stimulation, including frequent masturbation, is one of the behaviours demonstrated by captive chimps, who have also been found to display signs of trauma and depression similar to humans.

My friend Rosa has spent a good deal of time living in the forests of Sierra Leone studying the wild apes. There is a photograph of her smiling at a baby chimp held in her arms—Bruno. In the late 1980s, Rosa teamed up with Bala on a project to locate and count captive pet apes, and their findings underpinned the need for a sanctuary. There were fifty-five chimps living in people's houses in the capital Freetown alone, most of whom would have arrived as infants after their parents had been killed. People in Sierra Leone didn't used to hunt chimps. Local folklore says that chimps were once human—men and women transformed into apes as punishment for breaking the laws of the gods by fishing out of season. In my family's village of Rogbonko, hurting or hunting the monkeys that live in the trees whose branches bend over the river is forbidden. Many of the old beliefs had their roots in food conservation. In the dry season, the waters are low and fish scarce, the breeding season yet to begin. Back in the day, the priestess would have issued warnings against those minded to break her injunction—that to anger the gods was to risk being turned into apes—and then hoped people believed her. Some say people began to hunt apes for meat during the rebel war; others blame the Liberian rebels, who did not share our eating restrictions. I see something else: the rise of the evangelical preachers in the latter part of the twentieth century, the cold reach of Christianity, and its teachings of man's dominion over all animals.

The abandoned and abused chimpanzees that Bala and Rosa accepted into the new sanctuary would remain there the rest of their lives. Returning a formerly captive ape into the wild almost never works, Rosa told me, for the reason that wild ape troops carve the forest into territories, the boundaries of which are rigidly and violently enforced. Think of the forest like farmland, which can produce enough food to support a family of a certain size, then remember what humans have done in order to protect their land, or to seize it in the first place. To survive, a newly released ape—which would have had to be taught how to feed itself—would need to be accepted into a troop of wild apes without upsetting the existing hierarchy.

Rosa and I have a standing joke about our shared tendency to a mild form of misanthropy, a frustration with the shortcomings of our own species. Once, I gave her the gift of a vanity mirror I'd found in a gift shop in Covent Garden, *Do I look like a fucking people person?* written on the back. Now I remember something else Rosa said to me about chimps, her expression as she spoke, the slight shrug of the shoulders that seemed to suggest that what she was about to say was an unavoidable truth. 'They are us.'

And being like us has been the curse of the chimpanzee. Scientific experimentation on chimpanzees began in the 1920s when researchers purchased animals brought back to the US by hunters from West Africa. Around the same time, chimpanzees started to appear as the comic sidekick in Hollywood movies. Cheetah from *Tarzan* first appeared in a movie in 1932, although there were no chimpanzees in the original Edgar Rice Burroughs novels. Two years earlier, the first primate research centre in the United States was founded by the psychologist Robert Yerkes. Over the decades that followed, our attitude to chimpanzee experiments has changed. Writing

in 1989, Jane Goodall, calling for an end to ape experimentation, described the chimpanzee as a '*being* . . . whose emotional states are quite similar to our own and who is capable
of feeling pain, sorrow, happiness; a being who can trust and
whose trust is very easy to betray.' Today several countries have
banned ape experimentation, beginning with New Zealand
in 2000. In the United States (the largest user of apes for
scientific research), the National Institutes of Health, in 2013,
began to retire the majority of its research chimps, and soon
afterwards the US Fish and Wildlife Service announced that
it had designated captive chimpanzees an endangered species.
Cheetah had become Caesar.

Like us, chimps form close and enduring friendships,
their families held together by bonds of affection. In addition
to their intelligence and apparent humour, those qualities
that make people want to turn them into pets, chimps are,
like us, warmongering and homicidal. There are more attacks
on humans by captive chimps than wild chimps, though the
answer may rest in relative proximity and thereby opportunity, also the fact that wild chimps have learned to flee from
hunters and so humans in general. Bruno remained deeply
attached to Bala and later yearned for him. Who knows if
throwing rocks at human visitors was just the behaviour
of a protective alpha or bound to some deeper distrust of
humans?

In February 2013, I was invited to assist with a fundraiser
for the Tacugama Sanctuary in London. Jane Goodall was
there and so was Bala, alongside Paul Glynn, the author of
a children's novel about Bruno, the sale of which was going
to raise funds. A few years earlier the sanctuary had made

news in Sierra Leone and beyond. Something dramatic had
happened. Led by Bruno, the chimps had staged a breakout.
Bruno had escaped.

Tacugama Chimpanzee Sanctuary is reached by a long, narrow road, bordered by dense vegetation, which climbs steadily
toward the summit of a low hill. Today there is a visitors'
centre and a path through the trees that leads to the building
where the newly rescued chimps are sheltered before they are
introduced to the group. The roof of the building serves as
a vantage point out over a compound where the long-term
residents relax, eat and play. Beyond that lie many acres of
fenced forest where the chimps will eventually live out the
rest of their lives. In 2000, when I made my first visit, and
in 2006, which was the year the chimps escaped, the whole
place was much more modest than it is now: some cages, the
compound and a smaller parcel of forest.

Somehow the chimps succeeded in opening the gates to
the inner compound. Details of what happened overlap, vary
and sometimes contradict, but the essence of the story is the
same. The chimps raced down the access road toward the
Regent Road, which serves traffic to and from the capital. At
that moment on the Regent Road, a taxi was passing, carrying
two Americans and a Canadian; the men were contractors
working on the building of the new American embassy. The
driver was a local man, Issa Kanu. The visitors later recounted
the story of a huge ape that materialized out of the bush and
began to chase and then pound on the car. Issa Kanu tried
to reverse away but misjudged the road and crashed. He left
the vehicle. Or he was hauled out through the window by the

enraged chimp. Another version of the story has Issa Kanu
waiting alone outside the main gates of the sanctuary for the
foreigners who had gone inside in hopes of an early-morning
tour, and in so doing inadvertently released the apes who had
already escaped their compound.

What is not disputed is that Issa Kanu was killed, his
face and throat torn away. At first, news of the death was
withheld by the authorities. When it came to light, Bruno
was blamed, but by then the story of Bruno, who had still
not been recaptured, was taking on the cloak of fable. Bruno's
defenders pointed to another of the larger males called Phillip,
who had returned to the sanctuary and replaced Bruno as
the new alpha. The identity of the killer remains a mystery
because there were no witnesses who would have been able to
tell the apes apart.

Police and soldiers were brought in to search the surrounding forest. The government warned villagers to keep
their children indoors. Within days, many of the thirty-one
escapees had returned of their own volition and most of the
remainder were rounded up. Four remained at large. And
of the four, one was Bruno. Bounty hunters in 4x4s drove
out of the city, intent on bringing him down. There were
rumours of sightings, reports Bruno had been heard at night
hooting in the hills, whispers he had been killed. Nothing
was confirmed. The longer Bruno evaded his hunters, the
more intense the speculation grew. In 2006 I was home,
and I remember all talk was of Bruno: at weddings, in the
marketplace. The papers devoted daily coverage to the hunt.
People wore T-shirts: *I ♡ Bruno*. At a party, Rosa got into
an argument with an expat who thought it fun to sport a

T-shirt: *I Shot Bruno*. Bruno, the simian Spartacus, had the country rooting for him. In the years that followed, reports grew fewer. There came the occasional report of a sighting, but Bruno was never captured.

In 2017 my husband and I took our son to Sierra Leone for the first time. The rains that year were relentless. The traffic into the city was at a standstill, the beaches empty. One day we went to Tacugama, where we waited in the shelter of the visitors' centre for our escort, and then made our way under sighing trees that dripped with rainwater to the viewing place. Some of the younger apes turned their backs and bent over to show us their arses; one pitched shit from the mound of a distant rock. Directly below, in their pens, the newly arrived apes howled and keened. My son seemed to be looking at everything but the apes we had come to see.

A room behind us contained a small display, mainly posters telling of Tacugama's founding and the dreadful plight of apes in Sierra Leone, who, when they are not hunted as food, are losing their forest thousands of hectares at a time, sometimes to farmland for villagers but more often to industrial-scale farming by international companies. On one wall I found a picture of me taken at the London fundraiser. I showed my son, who turned to our guide: 'There's my mum.' The man looked at me and at the image on the wall. 'Ah,' he said and smiled for the first time.

I described our visit in 2000 and how Bruno had thrown rocks at us. In turn, he told me that he had been one of the first to join the sanctuary as a keeper. Face to face with him for the first time, I noticed his lazy eye.

'It was you,' I said. 'You were the one who showed us around.'

We shook hands, and he called to another keeper, who came over and examined the picture and then me and shook my hand also. He referred to the first man as Pa Moses and told us Pa Moses had trained him. I asked Pa Moses what he thought had happened the day the apes escaped.

'They would call to them, you see, madam,' the wild apes whose territories in the surrounding forest bordered the sanctuary. Some days an older female, whom the keepers named Congo, even ventured to sit on the other side of the perimeter fence and touch fingers with the apes inside. Sometimes she brought a baby with her and held it out for them to touch. Whether she was an emissary of sorts nobody knew, but the calls of the free apes, which came mostly at night, made the keepers uneasy because the apes in their care became agitated when they heard the cries. Still, no one saw the breakout coming. The keepers who fed the chimps and cleaned the enclosure entered and left through a double security gate; you had to secure the latch on one gate before you opened the next. The chimpanzees escaped through those gates. Some reports claimed the gates had been left unlatched. Pa Moses wasn't there that day, but he has his own theory. 'They watched us. Maybe they had been watching for months. They saw how it worked.'

Freedom would be tough for Bruno, for no alpha would accept another alpha into their troop. Bruno would have to found a new colony, perhaps somewhere distant. That would be hard, but not impossible, said Pa Moses. For chimps can travel long distances, and when they do, they don't swing through the trees but run on the ground, covering many miles in a day. 'The three who escaped with Bruno were the strongest of the males. Bruno took with him his best lieutenants. If any of the Tacugama apes could survive,' said Pa Moses, 'it would be those four.'

Later, when we mention to people in Freetown that we visited the ape sanctuary, everyone responds the same way, down to the shake of the head and little tsk: 'Bruno. He escaped them all.' And then they chuckle. They mean the posses who went after him, the police, the soldiers, the hunters. I listen and wonder how one ape came to mean so much to us because people here, whilst not unkindly, are rarely sentimental about animals.

Rosa says Bruno's legend had begun before the war: visitors to the sanctuary were fascinated by the chimps, and schoolchildren arrived each day by the busload. Bruno, with his might and size, instilled awe. War came, and the sanctuary was overrun by rebel soldiers twice, though the chimps amazingly survived; Bala and Pa Moses risked death to bring food to them. With the end of the war, Bruno's escape was the culmination of all that had happened, the end of the story. We were desperate for heroes in that time, for the truth of war is that there is no glory there. 'He became the embodiment of things coming right,' Rosa wrote to me years later.

When I ask my son, who has never known war, what he likes so much about the story of Bruno, he says he doesn't know. What if it had a different ending? I press. What if Bruno had returned to the sanctuary where he would be looked after for the rest of his life? My son frowns and shakes his head.

How soon do we learn it—the desire for autonomy? Bruno remained deeply attached to Bala, loved him, you might even say. We crave freedom even from those who love us and whom we love in return; it is a never-ending conflict of the soul. My son wants to be free of me yet knows he cannot live without me. The last time we talked about Bruno, I asked what else he liked about the story: 'What about the part when Bruno threw the rock at me?'

My son laughs, not his belly laugh, but a low, quiet laugh, like the broadening of a smile. 'Yes,' he said. 'I really like that bit too.'

The Peanut Butter Thief

I saw a thief. In Whole Foods, the man had been standing in line, waiting while the person ahead of him filled a container with peanut butter. When the turn of the thief came, he ignored the plastic tubs and instead traced swirls of peanut butter into the palm of an upturned hand. Then he turned around and saw me watching him.

I had been in Whole Foods less than ten minutes, enough time to choose and reject various styles of tomatoes: loose, on the vine or boxed, plum, grape, greenhouse, organic, cherry, Kumato, regular organic. *Regular* organic? I don't know what that means. The tomatoes were between three and five dollars a pack. I have already discussed with my son the cost of the pre-prepared watermelon he thinks he needs at $4.46 for the tub. Only if he promises to eat the lot, I say. And he promises and so he will be served watermelon at breakfast every morning of the coming week. Food in Arlington is expensive, more so than in London. When we arrived to live here we thought we were coming to the land of the free, or at least the comparatively inexpensive. Instead our monthly grocery bill is about a third higher than in London. A good many of our American friends find this hard to believe, such is the myth of low-cost USA. Other American friends told us about Costco; we go to Safeway for cereal, yoghurt and bagels, Whole Foods only for fresh produce. When I first lived in America in the nineties and Whole Foods was new, people used to call it Whole Paycheck. Whole Foods Market Peanut Butter Stock Roasted Organic costs $4.99 a pound, plus tax.

Americans eat three pounds of peanut butter each every year, which is apparently enough to coat the floor of the Grand Canyon. The average American child, unless they are allergic, will eat fifteen hundred peanut butter sandwiches by the time he or she graduates high school. Americans love peanut butter so much they have elected two peanut-growing presidents, Thomas Jefferson and Jimmy Carter. Across Europe and Asia, people don't care much for peanut butter; American peanut farmers complain about their inability to penetrate that market. For my part, I have never seen a French person eat peanut butter, but then the French have Nutella. I digress. George Washington Carver, a Black man, has been credited with the invention of peanut butter, though a farmer and promoter of the power of peanuts, the inventor (by which we mean here the first person to patent peanut butter) was a Canadian, Marcellus Gilmore Edson, which is perfectly plausible because Canadians are the only people who eat as much peanut butter as Americans. Way back, the Aztecs ground peanuts into a paste but failed to patent the results. The only other place I have known peanut butter consumed is West Africa. West Africans don't spread their butter on bread, because for the most part we don't eat much bread. We use it in cooking, in one of the most popular national dishes: groundnut stew.

Unless you are overweight (or, again, allergic), peanut butter is good for you, a high nutritional-value food. Commercially produced peanut butters may contain hydrogenated oils, palm oil, sugar or artificial sweeteners, and they almost always contain way too much salt. The best peanut butter should contain nothing but peanuts. Whole Foods freshly ground peanut butter is the liquid gold of peanut butters. Peanut butter is rich in monounsaturated fats. Two tablespoons of peanut butter contain eight grams of protein and up to three of fibre as well as niacin, iron, potassium and vitamin E. There's a good reason poor people feed their children peanut butter. Peanut butter was a staple of the government surplus food programme, by which the USDA used to buy up surplus commodities and either sell them at low prices to impoverished Americans or donate them to food banks. In the last decade food prices have soared—a combination of fuel prices and, some say, commodities speculation on the stock market. Surpluses have dried up.

Less than a year later, during the COVID-19 pandemic and when America had already been locked down for two months, I packed up jars of peanut butter; not peanut butter from Whole Foods, which I have never bought, but huge jars of Jif from Costco, for a food drive being organised by a neighbour. On the television we saw lines of cars at food banks. The drivers flipped open the boot; volunteers in masks and gloves placed boxes of donations directly inside. The camera, overhead in a news helicopter, panned down the length of cars which seemed endless. It was the vehicles that draw the eye:

big, shiny, SUVs, for the visual and intellectual dissonance
they presented. Are these people poor? A friend in Nigeria
writes to me via social media: 'We watch what's happening
in America with great interest and surprise.'

These Americans were not what aid agencies might call
'multi-dimensionally' poor, which is what you are when everyone you know is poor, and you have no access to education,
healthcare, clean water or jobs. However, one might think of
them as at least bi-dimensionally poor, having lost their jobs
and thereby their healthcare. Living in America, I heard for
the first time the word 'furlough' and during the COVID-19
emergency I witnessed the practise on a wide scale. Unlike the
multi-dimensional poor, though, the people in the line have
had access to credit with which they have bought these cars,
and before that probably their education. As a result of all
this, they have little or no savings. Their lives are like houses
on stilts now in the face of a typhoon.

The thief wore dirty Converse sneakers, a green army
jacket. His hair, thin and grey, reached the back of his collar.
When he turned I saw the tinge of stubble, the sag of skin
below his cheekbones. He saw me there and he knew that I
knew, and he stopped, like the fox that crosses my lawn and
suddenly spots me sitting on my stoop. I looked but did not
move or speak. A moment later he turned and walked away
and out of the door, hand upturned and full of peanut butter.

Wilder Things

The Vixen

Every year for the eighteen years we lived in our house in Waller Road, the vixen used our garden to raise her cubs. We called her '*the* vixen,' though I suppose there must have been more than one vixen because the life of an urban fox is typically short. The week Simon and I moved in, a neighbour told us about our resident fox and referred to her as '*the* vixen,' as if there had only ever been one. She'd had her den in our garden, but that would be the last year she did, for we had moved in with a dog, a lurcher, and lurchers are a hunting breed. We also tidied the garden, cut down the grass which grew to mid-thigh, pulled out the thicket of brambles and ivy and dismantled the rotting wooden shed, which I guessed had most likely sheltered her den. I saw her often that first summer, either crouching on the roof of the shed which stood in next door's garden or sitting in the long grass there. She would watch me battling the tap roots of the borage which had invaded our garden. When I turned away or went inside, she would dash across our garden, slipping through the gaps in the boards of the old fence.

In London, once darkness has fallen, the sight of a fox trotting along the road or pavement, leaping over a boundary fence, stealing between parked cars or clearing the low wall into someone's front garden, is a common one. While many foxes are naturally cautious, others are unfazed by the humans with whom they share the city. I have seen a fox waiting to cross a road in Piccadilly in the middle of the day. I have seen a fox trot past the guards outside Buckingham Palace. Countless times have I walked up the road on my way home from the Tube station behind a fox as it weaves its way around the other commuters. Once I saw a man checking his phone for messages, a fox crouched on a wall inches above him. The fox could have stretched out its paw and patted him on the head.

With the arrival of the winter months, our vixen began looking for a mate. If you have never heard the mating call of a fox, it is a lot like the sound of babies being murdered. I don't remember what I was doing the first time I heard the cry, but I do remember that I stopped and crossed to the window, opened it and listened. Only when I had decided the sound was not human did I close it again. One night in Waller Road the screams seemed to be coming from below our window. Our bedroom faced the street. I looked out to see the vixen cornered in our front garden, just a few feet of ground enclosed by a high privet hedge beyond which circled three adult male foxes. It looked as if, having gone out to find her new mate, our vixen was now faced with an embarrassment of riches. Simon ran downstairs, opened the front door and shooed the males, but to little effect. One hid behind a car. Another jumped the wall into the front garden of a house opposite. The third trotted some way up the road and kept watch at a safe distance. Still, the vixen took advantage of the distraction, slipped from her hiding place and was gone.

In the middle of the third night of screaming I lay awake and thought, Make your mind up, girl. Her last mate must have died or been killed, probably by a car, as many urban foxes are, because foxes usually mate for life. A day or so on I saw a large dog fox dozing in the sun on top of the neighbour's garden shed. A moment later the vixen jumped up and settled on her haunches next to him. He raised his head, she stretched out her neck, they touched noses and he reclined once more. The vixen had made her choice.

In the early spring we had the old fence replaced, and so for a while the foxes were forced to skirt our garden. In summer the cubs appeared, three of them; I would see them playing on the lawn in our garden. They knew about the dog and the sound of a window opening or a doorknob turning would send them scattering. One day I found, behind a forsythia bush, a small gap in the new fence, as though someone had nudged aside one of the boards. Since then, over the years we have owned the house, I have always made sure the gap remains and is kept clear. It is the fox run.

One morning I found a whole fox brush, burnished and lush, upon the grass. I picked it up to carry into the house for closer inspection, spied a giant flea and dropped it again. The brush had been bitten off right where it would have connected to the fox's body. It must have been a hell of a fight, with another fox I could only guess, because there were no dogs except mine. The most likely explanation is that a fox had trespassed on the vixen and her mate's territory and this tail belonged to the presumptive loser.

Whenever I saw the vixen or her cubs, I stopped whatever I was doing and watched. I thought unabashedly of love. I loved them for their gift of wildness and for bringing it to the city, to me in my garden, for the determination with which they faced the challenge of survival. For their beauty. I liked the way they ruffled the surface of life in the city. A plastic bag floating on the surface of a still lake is the sullying fingerprint of man on nature. A fox in the city is nature's act of resistance.

A good many people disagree with me. The British tabloid newspapers for one. Foxes stand accused of many crimes: raiding rubbish bins, spreading disease, attacking small dogs and cats. Very occasionally a fox bites a child. Year on year there is a call from someone for a fox cull, which is met by equally loud voices raised in opposition from fox lovers. So far there never has been a mass slaughter of London foxes. The truth is that it would never work. Trying to displace foxes is like trying to displace water, kill one and another will move into its territory.

The other truth is that foxes cause very little bother to the human inhabitants of the city and virtually no threat. They do not steal, because animals do not share our moral code, but they will take food from open dustbins. We all know, without needing to see statistical proof, that more children are bitten by dogs, cats, hamsters and each other than by foxes. Foxes carry mange but the chances of transmitting mange to a pet animal is extremely slight; on the other hand sarcoptic mange can devastate a fox population. The foxes leave turds on my lawn which my dog liked to rub her face into. Now *that* can be a nuisance, but nuisance is all.

What bothers people about foxes is that they will not be controlled and humans are control junkies. We love an ordered environment and there is none more so than the city. Here we are protected from the elements by concrete, brick, glass and steel. The streets are lit after night, so that we, the denizens of the city, do not trip or fall down holes should any holes alarmingly appear in the smoothed surfaces of the roads and walkways. Fresh water is piped into our homes, our waste is sluiced away. The great metropolises represent man's dominion over whatever in nature might cause us hurt or harm or discomfort. In Western nations we have lived this way so long we have become fearful of what is chaotic, the uncontrolled and uncontrollable. We do not care to be reminded that we are living beings, for that is to remember that we are vulnerable.

We tolerate animals only on our own terms. Mutualism is the existence in nature of a relationship that benefits both parties, the crocodile and the plover bird, for instance. The plover bird picks clean the teeth of the crocodile, who in turn does not snap its mouth shut. Dogs started out as wolves who entered a symbiotic relationship with man, helping to bring down big game in return for a place by the fire. Stephen Budiansky, author of *The Covenant of the Wild: Why Animals Chose Domestication*, argues that all our farm and food animals started out this way. But here is the fox, a creature that chooses to live close to humans but refuses subordination, has submitted neither to domestication nor taming, will not bend to anyone's will. The urban fox possesses a seeming irreverence

for both humans and our safe spaces. Those of us who find
beauty in urban foxes do so for the same reason their presence
provokes anger in so many, we admire and envy the foxes for
their defiance, for choosing freedom over safety.

One day, walking with my lurchers—by then we had two—I
saw a skinny adolescent fox with an unconcerned air slip
between the railings of the upper park. I paused a moment
and waited until it was out of sight. Neither dog had spotted
it. I was on crutches at the time, having broken my Achilles
tendon. I moved slowly and I didn't want to be pulled over by
the younger, keener and more unruly dog who still walked
on the lead. At the gate of the park I let her off and hobbled up
the hill to where there is a panorama of the city. Suddenly the
fox appeared from behind a bush. In a moment the younger
dog was upon it. I can tend to a Darwinian view, but this was
lunchtime and there were schoolchildren in the park, as well
as parents with toddlers. The fox ran for its life, but even so
the dog, faster and vastly taller, was over it in seconds, jaws
agape, teeth inches from the back of the fox's neck, waiting
only for the right moment to close her jaws, to flip the fox over
and crush its jugular. There's a place in the park where the
path narrows and then opens out onto a smaller section. The
dog and the fox had nearly completed a loop of the smaller
when the fox straightened its course, seeming to decide that
its best hope lay in the open park. I positioned myself at a
point in the path that bridged the two spaces and when the
pair passed me, I hurled myself upon them. The dog lost its
advantage, the fox made its escape.

All of this happened on the day in 2004 when the fox
hunting ban passed through the British Parliament. In the

years that followed some people wondered whether the ban had encouraged a growth in the urban fox population, that all these extra foxes were making their way into the cities. This is certainly untrue. Foxes have been drawn to and living in cities like London for many decades.

Our house on Waller Road is in New Cross Gate in South East London. Like all the houses on the surrounding streets, it was built by the Haberdasher's Guild towards the close of the nineteenth century. These spacious Victorian houses with equally large back gardens were rented to its members. In those days it was a genteel neighbourhood, but in the seventies, after the Guild began selling off its housing stock, the area fell into decline, mirroring the general downward trend of South East London, which had started during the Second World War. Into the neglected gardens and from the railway sidings where they had tended to live, moved the foxes.

In the 1970s came the Southwark slum clearances. In place of the tiny and unsanitary terraced homes were built the tower blocks that now hover over the lower reaches of the Old Kent Road (cheapest property on British Monopoly boards), which links South East London to the city and to Dover and the English Channel. From a rural road with a few wayside inns, in the nineteenth century, the Old Kent Road began to transform into an industrial centre with tanneries and factories. In 1833, the Metropolitan Gas Works were built. The huge metal gasholders now lie disused and the industrial lots have been turned into outlets for Carpetright, Carphone Warehouse, Pets at Home, McDonald's and Kentucky Fried Chicken. The smaller shops that line the road are mainly family-owned supermarkets and takeaways. On Friday and Saturday nights, young people travel in from Kent for the London club scene.

Often they stop for a takeaway on their way home, so by early morning the street sweepers are out, cleaning up the discarded boxes, the burger buns and chicken bones. But long before the street sweepers arrive, the foxes will have been, the rats and pigeons too. For them the city streets are an 'all you can eat' buffet. Free food and easy accommodation are what brought the foxes into London. They are here because of us.

In London, in the first decade of the new century, we had snow during consecutive winters. These were my insomniac years. Our oldest lurcher was by then blind. In the early hours of one February morning I woke to discover it had snowed. I dressed, pulled on my boots and fetched the old dog from her bed. She loved the cold, was forever plunging into the freezing waters of the North Sea, preferred to take her walks in wind and rain. Outside the snow was radiant, reflecting the glow of the streetlights. We headed uphill in the direction of the park. Though the snow reached the dog's flanks, she moved unhesitatingly onward for the first time in months, sensing the stillness, the absence of traffic, people or other dogs. We were entirely alone, all except for a fox walking up the hill ahead of us. It might have been our vixen, or some other fox with a nearby territory. She was walking up the centre of the road. Once she turned and looked at us, and then a little later she stopped, sat on her haunches and waited several seconds before setting off again. It looked for all the world as if she was assuring herself of our clumsy progress, the sleep-lorn woman and the blind dog. A naturalist would later tell me that when foxes do this they are checking to be sure we pose no threat. Evidently, she decided we did not, for she did not hasten her pace or seek the cover of the shadows. She slipped between the railings of the park and next moment she was gone.

An American Success Story

The first time I saw a coyote was in Death Valley in California on a road trip from Tucson to San Francisco in the early years of my marriage. We had come to live in the United States for a year while I was on a fellowship at Berkeley. Around a bend we came upon an animal standing in the middle of the road. My husband slowed and then stopped the car. The coyote was looking at us with an unruffled curiosity. She trotted around to the passenger side, cocked her head slightly and looked me dead in the eye. The behaviour, which at first had struck us as odd (was she rabid?) seemed suddenly familiar. I recognised it from our dog back home. I said: 'She's begging!' Not wishing to encourage her, we drove on.

My second coyote encounter was out horse riding in Wyoming, months later. There came the sound of laughter: the high-pitched and breathless hysterics of a gaggle of schoolchildren let loose with a canister of helium. The young woman leading our ride held up her hand and we halted. My horse's ears twitched, the nervous roll of an eye. 'Coyotes. Coming this way. Prepare to loose your horses.' Everyone dismounted, freed the reins and held on to our horses' bridles. The coyote pack sounded like a big one, maybe two dozen. It's hard, though, to tell with coyotes; the multiple notes of their calls might emanate from two or ten. Either way, if the horses bolted, we were told it was better to let them go. They would head back to their stables, five or six miles down the mountain.

We'd have to make our own way on foot. The calls grew louder and then faded. The horses settled. We remounted and moved on.

Many years later, in 2011 and 2013, I taught at Williams College in Williamstown, Massachusetts. Williamstown is a small, attractive village of eight thousand near the Vermont border. The Taconic Ridge lies to the north-west on the New York–Massachusetts border, Mount Greylock rises to the south-east, forming part of the Appalachian Trail which slips past to the east of the town. There is a fluid beauty to the tree-covered landscape, shifting with the seasons, the most popular of which is the fall, whose colours thousands travel here to see. In nearby North Adams the abandoned warehouses and dilapidated homes give testament to the decline in the region's industry, the mills that once produced lumber, grist, paper and textiles. Today the wealthy who keep second homes in and around Williamstown are more likely to have made their money in the financial markets. They are attracted by the beauty of the town's surrounds and also by the summer theatre festival, the Clark Art Institute and MASS MoCA, which opened in an empty North Adams factory in 1999.

As in many small towns in rural America, animal encounters are a way of life in Williamstown. One morning, a report reached us that a bear had been seen outside the middle-school gates. The bear was leaning against a car, as though it were waiting there for someone, got tired and decided to take the weight off his feet. One night, sitting on my back porch with friends from Sweden, we saw an animal none of us recognised walking in the road. From Google we learned the creature was a fisher. On the outskirts of North Adams, a moose had been spotted several times near the same crossroads. And on other days, I found scats on my lawn that looked as though a dog had gorged itself upon a bowl of cherries. When I noticed similar scats in the grounds above the Clark Institute, I consulted a wildlife tracking manual. The scats matched those of the coyote.

Stephen DeStefano is a wildlife biologist and author of *Coyote at the Kitchen Door*, a book I had come across while living in Williamstown. I discovered he lived a three-hour drive away towards Boston and arranged to meet him for lunch in the pretty tourist town of Sheldon Falls one day in late November. When I arrived, the sky was silver-grey, swollen with coming snow. DeStefano looks how you'd expect a man in his line of work to look—he wore a heavy beard and a baseball cap and drove a Toyota pickup. His field of expertise is known in the world of the wildlife biologist as animal-human co-existence, or sometimes animal-human conflict, depending on your take. Stephen is a member of Massachusetts Large Animal Response Team, the person you call if you have a bear outside the school gates. In his book, he gives an account of being called out by a farmer who had found a moose calf in his horse paddock. Stephen and his team tranquillise the animal with the intention of removing her to safety, only to attract a growing crowd of onlookers from a nearby town when a local news announcer broadcasts the story. In the book, DeStefano chides himself for a faint impatience towards these well-meaning folk, a result of his frustration with certain public attitudes: 'I worry about the concentration of people here in Massachusetts, the number of roads, the ceaseless encroachment of development, and maybe most of all the alarming nonchalance of many of the state's residents toward the spread of the built environment.'

Of all North America's large mammals, the coyote produces the greatest range of emotions. To America's original inhabitants, the coyote is God's Dog, a semi-divine creature, capable of assuming human form. In Native American stories the coyote is sometime Creator, who gifts humans fire and daylight and teaches them wisdom, and sometime trickster, one who continually transgresses moral boundaries. To farmers past and present, coyotes are a menace to livestock. To hikers and dog walkers they are an unnerving and largely unwelcome presence. To town dwellers the coyote is a threat to small children, the chief suspect behind missing cats and small dogs.

Coyotes originated on the prairies of the Great Plains and the Great Basin Desert, Stephen explained over lunch. A couple of hundred years ago that was the only place you found them. But then something changed. The coyotes began to leave the plains, spreading north-west through Oregon and Washington State, east across Wyoming and Montana, the Midwest and New England, all the way to the Eastern Seaboard. From dry plains to snow-covered mountains, from creosote bush to hemlock forests, from one hundred plus degrees Fahrenheit to five. I had seen evidence of coyotes in places along that very migratory arc. Coyotes are one of the most adaptable and resilient creatures in North America ever. Stephen calls them 'an American success story.'

'They are wild creatures who are also wholly adapted to the suburban and urban environment,' said Stephen. 'They eat everything and can live anywhere.' Desert coyote feed almost exclusively on small animals, voles and mice, but once coyotes left the desert and began the long march north and east they learned to make a meal of whatever was available, from windfall apples and soft fruit to roadkill. The scat I saw in my garden was likely of a coyote that had fed on 'somebody's late summer garden crop.'

In New England, when coyotes first began to be sighted, people thought they were wolves. Not the great grey wolf, which had long been extirpated from the state, but a smaller, fleeter wolf which they called variously a brush, timber or prairie wolf. Others claimed they were wild dogs. Those few who recognised them as coyote thought they must have been brought in as pets and abandoned. In 1972 one of the beasts was shot and carted into town on the flatbed of a pickup. Too small for a wolf, too large for a coyote. A team from Hampshire College conducted a study on the carcasses of others hit by cars and concluded this was neither wolf nor dog nor coyote but an entirely new species. They named it the New Hampshire canid. More animals were captured and studied. Their paws did not sweat like those of coyotes, their snouts were longer and thinner, they stood taller at the shoulder, they did not form packs in the same way as wolves or hunt as wolves, yet their coats were more wolf-grey than red, and they seemed less afraid of humans than either coyotes or wolves. But the howl, the howl was the howl of a coyote. In the end, though different opinions continue to be debated, a conclusion was reached. The animals were coyotes that had somehow fast-tracked evolution. They called it the eastern coyote.

So what enabled the expansion in the coyote's territory and heralded their evolutionary leap forward? The answer is wolves, or more accurately, the absence thereof. From the earliest, pioneers to North America waged a ferocious war upon wolves. AR Harding's *Wolf and Coyote Trapping* (subtitled *An*

Up-to-Date Wolf Hunter's Guide, Giving the Most Successful Methods for Experienced 'Wolfers' for Hunting and Trapping These Animals, Also Gives their Habits in Detail), published in 1909, was the wolfer's bible and gives an account of the many ways in which wolves were brought to their deaths: they were shot, hunted, caught in steel-jawed leg traps and clubbed to death, poisoned with strychnine and cyanide.

The wolfers didn't just kill wolves that threatened livestock, they enacted a genocide on the entire species. Harding hails the day of the wolf's coming extermination and ascribes them human motivations, calling them 'cowardly,' 'destructive' and 'blood thirsty desperadoes.' In *Of Wolves and Men*, Barry Lopez details the way the animals were treated as outlaws and criminals, subjected to public torture and execution. Crowds gathered to watch a particular wolf die, as agonisingly as possible: drawn and quartered, hanged and left to swing on the gibbet. The bounty-hunting wolfers (paid for every pair of ears they turned in, a wolfer armed with traps and strychnine, could take hundreds of animals in a season) were treated as folk heroes. Strychnine causes the most painful of deaths. The animal's muscles contract and spasm, starting at the head and neck and gradually affecting the whole body. The convulsions worsen and never stop. The wolf eventually dies of asphyxiation caused by paralysis of the neural pathways that control breathing, or from sheer exhaustion.

So successful was the massacre of wolves that today they are a protected species, and, so now with human inconstancy, we revere that which we would have destroyed.

Into the void left by the wolf, in the landscape of both North America and the popular imagination, loped the coyote:

swagman, scavenger, clown, killer, conjurer, shapeshifter, vag-
abond, thief.

Often, when a coyote pack moves through a territory, they
walk in single file, one coyote takes the lead, the second places
its paw print in the exact same spot as the leader, the coyote
behind does the same and the coyote behind that one and so
on. The pack moves with a single pulse such that it looks as
if only one coyote has passed. I heard a story once about a
pack of coyotes and a group of hunters. The hunters had been
tracking the coyote all through the day and into the dusk,
until it was too dark to see, and so they rested and the next day
resumed the hunt at first light. This went on, the men alter-
nately tracked and rested. On the fourth day they came across
a second, older set of tracks and a short time later discovered
a set of human footprints which they soon recognised as their
own. One by one each man came to the same realisation. They
had been led in a circle over a wide terrain during which time
the pack had gradually closed the distance between them. The
coyote were now directly behind the men.

An apocryphal story perhaps, but it is based on an indis-
putable truth. Coyotes somehow survived the same treatment
that killed the wolves. Gary Snyder once wrote of Native
American coyote myths: 'Coyote never dies, he gets killed
plenty of times, but he always comes back to life.' Over recent
decades coyote numbers have multiplied. Nowadays coyotes
are in the hills, in the fields, in the suburbs, where they den
in railroad yards, under sheds, beneath the steps of abandoned
houses, on the edges of parking lots; they are in cities too.
Coyotes must count as one of the world's most resilient species.

Kill one coyote and another will take its place, kill many and coyotes will hyper-breed more and bigger litters of pups to replace their lost numbers. In the battle between man and coyote, the coyote is winning.

In Massachusetts, the summer after we first met, Stephen and I reprised the conversation begun in Sheldon Falls. This time we were walking in the woodland around his house in New Salem. Stephen was calling the names of trees and plants while I made notes: white birch, paper birch, yellow birch, mountain laurel, Eastern hemlock, American chestnut. He stopped to explain how the chestnuts had been destroyed by blight decades before and now never grew past a few feet. Bracken fern, ostrich fern, sensitive fern, sarsaparilla, Indian cucumber. He bent and touched a cluster of Indian pipe, bowed and spectrally pale. Calls for a coyote cull, he told me, come mainly from suburban moms, pet owners and hunters. The question of whether to hunt predators continues to divide biologists, but, said Stephen, and he stopped and turned to me, it's the wrong question: 'The key question is, do we have a real problem or do we just *think* we have a problem.'

The next week Stephen took me coyote calling. We left from his house in New Salem one day after dark. With us was Ki who is married to Stephen and is also a wildlife biologist. The fourth person in Stephen's Toyota was a BBC producer, Geoff, with whom I was making a radio documentary. We were headed for the Quabbin Reservoir, which provides drinking water for the whole of Boston and sits in a large tract of forested land. It is where Ki works managing biodiversity and a clean water supply.

Stephen had brought with him a predator caller, which some hunters use to lure their quarry. The caller contains recordings of prey animals in distress, injured birds say, or jackrabbits and the like. Some callers also contain recordings of the cries of lost or injured predator juveniles, coyote pups and mountain lion kittens, in the hope of luring the adult. You may make your own judgement about that. Anyway, for our purposes we were interested only in the coyote howler, which is the sound of a pack, the yips and screams of their night-time recitative. The equipment was new, and Stephen fiddled with it for a minute or two. Geoff, looking for a place to balance his microphone, wound down the window. The night air was soft, warm, still. The total absence of ambient light made it impossible to see more than a few feet into the darkness. From the moment Stephen shut off the engine we seemed to have been enfolded into a dark hush.

Stephen opened his own window, held the equipment aloft and turned it on. First came a howl, then a series of barks and yips. When they finished, we listened in the silence. Nothing. Stephen pressed the button again and the caller played a different series of coyote sounds. We waited. The return call came some seconds later, and from far closer than I had imagined; they must have been watching us since our arrival. A single coyote howl, then another and another. A string of yips. On Geoff's recording you can hear a small intake of breath from Ki and Stephen, who says: 'That's them!'

In 2015 I was staying in a small cabin called Meadow House on Whidbey Island in Puget Sound. One morning I rose early with the hope of sighting a coyote, though with insufficient conviction to bother to dress for the enterprise,

I was still in my nightwear and carrying my first cup of tea. The coyote stood entirely still, watching me from behind a tangle of rose hip, at such a distance that it could have been a tree stump, or it might have been a small deer. I took a step forward. With my second step the animal retreated, and I caught the distinctive roll of a coyote. Coyotes inhabit most of the North American islands. In Whidbey they are thought to have trotted over Deception Pass Bridge when it was built in the 1930s, but the presence of coyotes on many islands, such as those off Cape Cod, cannot be accounted for. Did they swim?

On another occasion, outside in search of a mobile-phone signal, I looked up and directly into the eyes of a coyote sitting in the meadow grass. The eyes were all I could see, the eyes and the outline of the ears, for the rest blended so perfectly with its background that it was impossible to say where the windblown grasses ended and the animal began. Neither of us blinked. I raised my phone to try to capture its image, and at the movement the coyote turned. Then I saw, emerging out of the grass in short, energetic bounds, one, two, three, four coyotes. Stephen DeStefano, when I wrote to him about my encounter, thought they were probably a family group, a mating pair with a couple of last year's female pups. The males would have left to find their own territories by that time of the year: 'It is one thing to see one, even close,' he wrote back. 'But it is special to make that eye contact.' It had happened to him just two or three times, the last being the encounter at his house in New Salem, when a coyote swung out of the woods and snatched one of Stephen and Ki's chickens while they were eating supper outdoors one warm summer evening, the encounter at the kitchen door.

Then in the spring of 2018, sitting on the back step of my house in Virginia, I looked once again into the eyes of a coyote. For a few seconds, as the animal and I regarded each other, I considered the possibility that this was a very large fox or someone's dog. But then it turned and trotted past me, and again there was the giveaway rocking gait.

A week or so later, a neighbour posted a photograph of a wild animal on the website Nextdoor. The coyote in the picture didn't look like the one I had seen. The fur was much darker. That meant there was at least a pair. Then early the following spring, another neighbour managed to get a photograph of a coyote and she, too, posted it on Nextdoor. Suzanne Peurachs is a wildlife biologist who had taken part in some of the early studies of coyote in the DC area. She described the experience of looking out of her window to see what her husband had said was a large dog standing by their gate: 'I had my eyes locked on the dog and suddenly it looked up, locked eyes with me, and it just disappeared. I saw nothing, it was there and then it was not.' Coyotes are new to north Virginia, the first were seen just twenty or so years ago. Now they are at my own kitchen door.

Cheeverville

The good people of North Arlington, VA, love their lawns. I have never seen lawns like it, not even in Britain, famous for its lawns. The grass is brashly green and longer than the British keep theirs, so that the lawns look like 1970s shagpile carpets. In Arlington, most people eschew fences, hedges or other boundary markers. In fact, in many places there are ordinances forbidding enclosing your front lawn in the interests of preserving a certain aesthetic. In the streets around where I live, the houses are perched, each atop a man-made hillock of excavated earth, and one neighbour's lawn rolls seamlessly into the next. From their drawing rooms the eye of the householder may roam across acres of uninterrupted green. If Capability Brown had been a suburban landscape designer, such views would become his trademark.

The lawn of the first house we lived in in Arlington when we moved here in 2015 was an exception to all this. The house was an old colonial, and the yard was heavily shaded, as were the yards on either side. One of our neighbours grew hostas and ferns. We grew nothing. The lawns of the cul-de-sac below, by contrast, were lovely. A few deer used our garden as a passage through to the cul-de-sac. When I was out smoking on the stoop of our covered porch in the evenings, a deer might emerge from the passage that ran down the side of the house and pass a few feet from me. Deer are not the dainty beasts they appear; they are quite heavy-footed. Once, when I was sitting out there in the dark, I heard an unfamiliar sound, a heavy dragging, quite unlike the regular hoof fall of a deer. I could see nothing through the darkness, only hear a hoarse breathing and again, this awful dragging sound as it grew louder. Whatever it was passed and I stood up to look after it into the street. It was an injured doe and the sound was of her dragging one of her hind legs.

In the yard we had a trampoline for our son, and in the spring as the weather grew warmer, a doe and her two new fawns liked to lie beneath it in the shade. Over time we all grew used to each other until it became possible for me to sit in companionable silence reading on the deck just a couple of dozen feet away. Arlington, like many counties in Virginia and in the DC area, in fact, a good deal of suburban America, is overrun with deer. County administrations are in constant search of solutions.

One cold morning I rose from my bed at 2 o'clock and drove an hour south-west of Arlington to Prince William County (population 402,000). The traffic on I-95 was mainly haulage vehicles—the few places that were open along the way cater to truck drivers. I was on my way to Locust Shade Park to meet a man called Purvis Dawson. Locust Shade Park is a pretty recreational ground with a boating pond, a mini golf course, a little outdoor amphitheatre and an abundance of deer. Purvis is a former police chief, a job he retired from in 2012, and is now Chief Park Ranger for Prince William County where he was piloting a project to cull suburban deer. The programme had started that season, this was one of the last shoots. I found Purvis waiting for me at the park gates. We sat in the warmth of his ranger's vehicle, and while we waited for the hunters to arrive, he told me how all past efforts made to curb the suburban deer population—from planting contraceptives in their feed to bringing in sharpshooters—had failed. This latest attempt used volunteer bowhunters (bows being less hazardous to the public than high-velocity rifles). 'There are more deer in Virginia today than in sixteen hundred,' said Purvis. And while householders vex over shrubbery and deer ticks, Purvis, who was once commander of animal services for Fairfax County, was more concerned about the damage to the environment by overgrazing and car accidents. *One and a half million people* drive their cars into a deer every year in the US.

The first pickup to arrive was driven by Jerry, leader of the Stafford Archers. Jerry was followed by Donny, David, Ronnie,

Dwayne, Eric. They were a truck driver, two mechanics and two IT specialists, respectively. Jerry was a road engineer. I was a little concerned they might be defensive around me, but everybody seemed relaxed. They talked about recent hunts, how the first time out they saw thirty deer and took ten, how the deer learned fast, because last week they saw only three and took none. Most of the hunters had spent the last week positioning cameras around the park, trying to figure out where the deer bed and where they grazed. Yesterday the men put up their stands, in which they would wait and watch until dawn had come and gone.

The men needed to get to their stands. Nobody invited me to join them and if they had, I would have said no. They'd already told me that their collective chances of taking any deer at all that day were extremely slight and I'd been deer-hunting once before; I know I lack the requisite patience and the circulatory efficiency to sit for several hours in the cold. Also, I was hungry. Ronnie pressed home-made venison jerky on me. He lives in Gum Springs in Alexandria and grew up with a father who hunted all the family's meat. He fed the people of Gum Springs with his bounty; the other hunters donated their share of the venison to homeless shelters. When I told Ronnie about the deer around my house, he offered to shoot them. All perfectly legal, he said, if I had a quarter acre. My garden was well placed because it lay adjacent to public land and though you can't shoot deer on public land, you can track onto it. 'Make a deal with a few of the neighbours,' he said, grinning because he was trying to get a rise out of me.

In Arlington, in our first house, our neighbours took differing views of the deer. The hosta people, who actually lost a great many hostas to the appetites of the deer, had an easy-come, easy-go attitude. But the woman in the newly built house in the cul-de-sac below us reserved a special loathing for the deer. It infuriated her, the way they wandered from our yard into hers. She did not want them doing damage to her newly laid turf. Deer don't much care to eat grass, except when it is young and succulent, which hers certainly was. I feel certain she did not like our laxity in allowing the deer to use our trampoline as a sunshade. One day she asked us to build a fence between our garden and hers. We explained we were renting, that she would need to contact the householders, who declined, and so she hired contractors and erected a fence at the bottom of our garden at her own expense. But the deer just walked around it, so gradually she sought permission from other neighbours and kept extending the fence in both directions until she had put up, in all, perhaps seventy foot of fence line.

Our second home in Arlington is on a street the kind of which I have never lived on before. I call it Cheeverville after the stories of John Cheever. People here have swimming pools and some have horseshoe driveways. And if you don't have your own pool, there is Donaldson Run swimming pool, a members-only neighbourhood pool close to our house. In the summer I see people walk down the street in bathing suits, wrapped in towels. A preponderance of Doric columns decorate the facades of the homes, as if the Parthenon has been dismantled and shipped here by the residents, whose average household income is over $200,000 a year.

Our house (no columns, no pool, nor horseshoe) borders the sixty-seven-acre Potomac Overlook Regional Park, one of the last few remaining woodlands in an area that was once forest. In it are the remains of several Native American settlements, two of which date back to prehistoric times and one to the nineteenth or twentieth century. According to the National Park Services website, forty years of contact with Europeans decimated the native populations of this part of Northern Virginia, most of whom died of diseases brought by the foreigners or else war. The survivors left to join other tribes. Today the population of Arlington is less than one per cent Native American.

A four-lane freeway runs the length of the north side of the park, on the other side is Donaldson Run swimming pool. Everywhere else it is surrounded by houses. At the top of the hill, near the entrance to the park, you find a basketball court, a playground and tennis courts. Next to these a stand of *Ailanthus altissima,* or Tree of Heaven, is being monitored by the park authorities. Tree of Heaven is an imported, invasive species, the bark and leaves of which produce a toxin that inhibits the growth of other trees. There is also a small nature centre, which my son loves to visit. Among the exhibits are stuffed animals: a threadbare black bear, a fox, a goose; a shop-soiled white swan circles overhead. A small outdoor enclosure houses injured raptors, all of whom—a red-tailed hawk and several owls—have been blinded after being hit by cars. The rangers who run the centre are young and enthusiastic. A young man called Casey tells me there are coyote in the woods, they have been caught on the park's security cameras. Not long ago he found a dead coyote on the side of the freeway where it borders the park.

A few days after my conversation with Casey, it snowed, and in the early morning I took my son out to look for animal tracks. The trees cast wraithlike shadows; the scarlet of the cardinals startled against a monochrome snowscape. Along the length of a fallen tree we found the elongated paw prints, the inward turned toes of a coyote and, a day later, in a hollow in the centre of the park, many dozens more. Not long afterwards, one weekday at dusk, and for the first time, I heard the sound of coyote calling. Coyote will sometimes 'pack up' (as naturalists say) and take down a deer, but coyote are not pure carnivores in the way of wolves and, with so much else on offer in suburbia, can't on the whole be bothered with the effort required of hunting deer. It was from the back stoop of this house, next to the park, that I had my most recent coyote sighting the following spring.

Even sharing with the coyote, the park is the only place the deer can call their own. Near the playground there is a board with a display 'Changes in the Land Through the Years.' It shows four black-and-white aerial images dated 1937, 1948, 1970 and 2000. In 1937 the area is largely woodland. Arrows point to Donaldson Farm and an orchard belonging to a Mrs White. The freeway hasn't been constructed yet, and the woods reach right up to the Potomac River. In 1948 the first development of houses is in the process of being built. The Donaldson Farm is gone. By 1970 there are hundreds of houses, they spread over two thirds of what twenty years before was woodland. The freeway, George Washington Parkway, has been built, and so has the swimming pool. Arlington is an inner-ring suburb—it takes just minutes to drive into the District, and its growth mirrors that of many American suburbs. Between 1940 and 1960, Arlington's population tripled from 57,000 to 163,000, coinciding with the middle-class exodus from DC, a direct result of school desegregation. Arlington did everything to resist desegregation, but in 1970 the city's battle with the federal legislative authorities culminated in

Black students being bussed in by court order. In the 1970s, Arlington fell into decline but rose again from 153,000 residents in 1980 to the 227,000 people who live here today. The last image on the board shows a new housing development in the bottom right-hand corner of the frame. And there, on the end of a row of houses and next to the first trees, is the home where we live.

During the fall, and from the window of my study, I watched the deer come to feed on the acorns from the oak tree next to our lawn. The largest herd comprises some does and more than a half a dozen fawns. One day, as I walked my son to catch the school bus, we saw them standing on the lawn of the house next to the stop, upon which the schoolchildren often play as they await the arrival of the bus. That day it looked as though our children had been turned, by a witch's wand, into creatures of the forest. There is, for me, an arresting otherworldliness to the sight of suburban deer, it is as though they have stepped through some wrinkle in time. A bachelor herd once emerged from the woods, three huge, muscular bucks, each crowned with a pair of new antlers and wearing a heavy winter coat, like lords of Cawdor.

Another time, walking around the neighbourhood, two women standing on the pavement ahead of me gestured and pointed to where several deer were emerging from a small stand of pines. A silver-haired couple, passing by, stopped at the sight of the deer but briefly. 'Giant mice,' said the man. To which his wife replied: 'They were here first!'

I remember the deer as they passed me while I sat on the stoop of our first house in Arlington. There was something spectral about their unhurried progress, their apparent obliviousness to my presence. I am reminded of a story I heard once about a legion of Roman centurions whose ghostly forms could sometimes be seen passing through the outer walls of a pub in a small Sussex town. The centurions, so the story goes, were marching along the route of an old Roman road which lay beneath the foundations of the public house.

The more I talked to people about the animals who live in our cities, the more I came across a particular stance which makes me uncomfortable. The people most exercised cite all the threats these creatures supposedly pose to us and to our safety, but not one has ever offered evidence of having been so threatened themselves, they only tell me what they have read or heard. This compulsive detailing of often incorrect data strikes me as an effort, perhaps subconscious, to conceal and at the same time to justify what perhaps they do not even recognise in themselves. Listening to them, I grew increasingly convinced their rage had existed for a long time and I suspected they raged at other things in their lives too. They hated the animals simply for being, for being in places which these people thought they owned and the animals had no right to be.

What would happen to the wildlife, I have often wondered, if by plague or alien attack the cities became emptied of human life? In *The World Without Us*, Alan Weisman speculates that within five hundred years, in a place like Arlington, the forest would have grown back the way it was, but with a few aluminium dishwasher parts and some stainless-steel cookware buried in the undergrowth. But what of the animal life? Far from being overrun by wildlife, my conversations with urban biologists suggest, the cities would be abandoned by the coyotes and foxes; rats, raccoons and pigeons would leave too. Those creatures are here only because we are here. The deer, however, would not leave, because this is their land and they would reclaim it, at least for as long as it took for the wolves to return. Gardens would grow fallow, borders cede to wildflowers, herds would gather on the overgrown lawns, rotted fences give way to erstwhile animal paths. And the injured doe, made anew, would walk the same tracks through the woods as deer have for hundreds of years.

Author's Note

In accordance with current practice I have capitalised the word Black. I have restricted capitalisation to occasions when I am referring to a specific racial, cultural and/or political category of minority peoples who identify and may be identified as such, namely Black American and Black British. On those occasions when I am referring to a person's or people's skin tone or appearance, or where the term is historically or socially irrelevant, I have used 'black.'

Acknowledgments

The Window Seat began thanks to a suggestion by my editor, John Freeman. I'm grateful to him for the vision he brought to selecting, out of the many essays I have written over the years, those which we could shape into a book which offers a particular view of the world, one which has been my life but I have rarely seen written. We have worked together for ten years. Good years all. He is responsible for commissioning and/or editing and publishing many of the pieces that appear here, namely "The Last Vet," "Ice," "1979," "Crossroads," "Power Walking," "What If You Gave an Inauguration and Nobody Came," "Bruno" and "Wilder Things." Thanks, John.

Thank you to the publisher of this collection, Morgan Entrekin, who has been a wonderful publisher and good friend, as has my agent, David Godwin. Thank you also to the Grove Atlantic team for bringing this project to fruition. I'm grateful to the Lannan Foundation, whose fellowship enabled my trip to Shetlands and Orkney, and to my brother, Gregor Prattley, who accompanied me there. People who have helped especially: Ellah P. Wakatama; Rosalind Hanson Alp; Gudush Jalloh; members of my family, the Scottish and the Sierra

Leonian, who appear in some of these essays; Simon Westcott and Mo Forna Westcott, my husband and my son.

The following essays originally appeared in other publications. Many have been the subject of minor revisions or additions and occasionally an anecdote may have appeared elsewhere in interviews, lectures or otherwise in my work. "Ice" was first published by *Literary Hub* as "The First Time I Saw Ice Was in the Jungle" in 2017. The essay "Obama and the Legacy of Africa's Renaissance Generation" appeared in 2018 in the *New York Review of Books Daily*, edited by Matt Seaton. "Santigi" was published in the *New Daughters of Africa: An International Anthology of Writing by Women of African Descent*, 2019, edited by Margaret Busby. "1979" was previously published in *Granta: After the War*, 2013, edited by John Freeman and Ellah P. Wakatama. "Technicals" appeared as part of the MOMA *Design and Violence* online exhibition curated by Paola Antonelli, 2013–2015, and was then selected for the print catalogue, which was published in 2015. "Crossroads" came out first in *Freeman's: Family*, 2016, edited by John Freeman. "The Last Vet," the earliest dated essay contained in this collection, was previously published in *Granta: Work* in 2010, edited by John Freeman and Ellah P. Wakatama. "Power Walking" first appeared in *Freeman's: Power*, 2018, edited by John Freeman. "What If You Gave an Inauguration and Nobody Came" was written for *Literary Hub* in 2018. The essay "Bruno" appeared first in *Brick* in 2020, edited by Allison LaSorda, and was republished in *Tales of Two Planets*, 2020, edited by John Freeman. "Wilder Things" appeared as a *Literary Hub* essay in 2018.